CBAP® & CCBA™ Exam Prep

ITO Diagrams

By Linda Erzah, CBAP

Copyright © 2012 BAMentor™

8343 Roswell Road Ste 144
Atlanta, GA 30350-2810
www.TheBAMentor.com

No part of this publication may be reproduced, stored in a retrieval system, or transmitted in any form of by any means, electronic, mechanical, photocopying, recording, scanning, or otherwise, except as permitted under Section 107 or 108 of the 1976 United States Copyright Act, without the prior written permission of the copyright holder.

Portions copyright by International Institute of Business Analysis (IIBA®). Materials are used with the express permission of International Institute of Business Analysis.

All trademarks or copyrights mentioned herein are the possession of their respective owners and BAMentor makes no claim or ownership by the mentioned that contain these marks.

BAMentor is an independent entity from International Institute of Business Analysis (IIBA®) and is only affiliated with IIBA® as an Endorsed Education Provider (EEP™).

IIBA®, the IIBA® logo, *BABOK*® and Business Analysis Body of Knowledge® are registered trademarks owned by International Institute of Business Analysis. These trademarks are used with the express permission of International Institute of Business Analysis.

CBAP® is a registered certification mark owned by International Institute of Business Analysis (IIBA®). This certification mark is used with the express permission of International Institute of Business Analysis.

CCBA™ is a trademark owned by International Institute of Business Analysis (IIBA®). This certification mark is used with the express permission of International Institute of Business Analysis.

Neither the IIBA® nor BAMentor warrant that use of this workbook will ensure passing the IIBA® certification exams.

Copyright © 2012 BAMentor™

Copyright © 2012 BAMentor™

Table of Content

Chapter 2: Business Analysis Planning & Monitoring 1
Chapter 3: Elicitation...8
Chapter 4: Requirements Management & Communication 13
Chapter 5: Enterprise Analysis 19
Chapter 6: Requirements Analysis 25
Chapter 7: Solution Assessment & Validation 32
Product Catalog..39

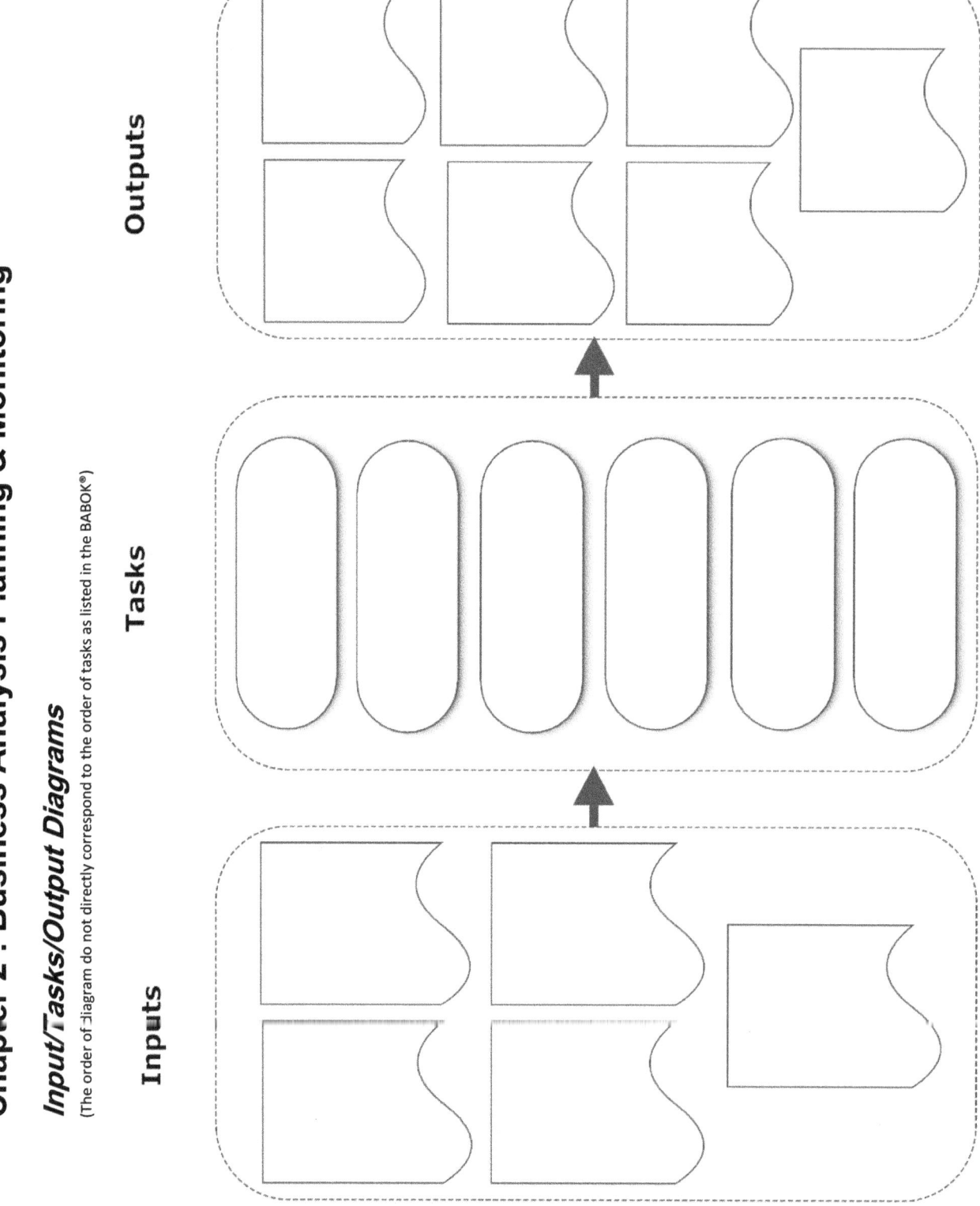

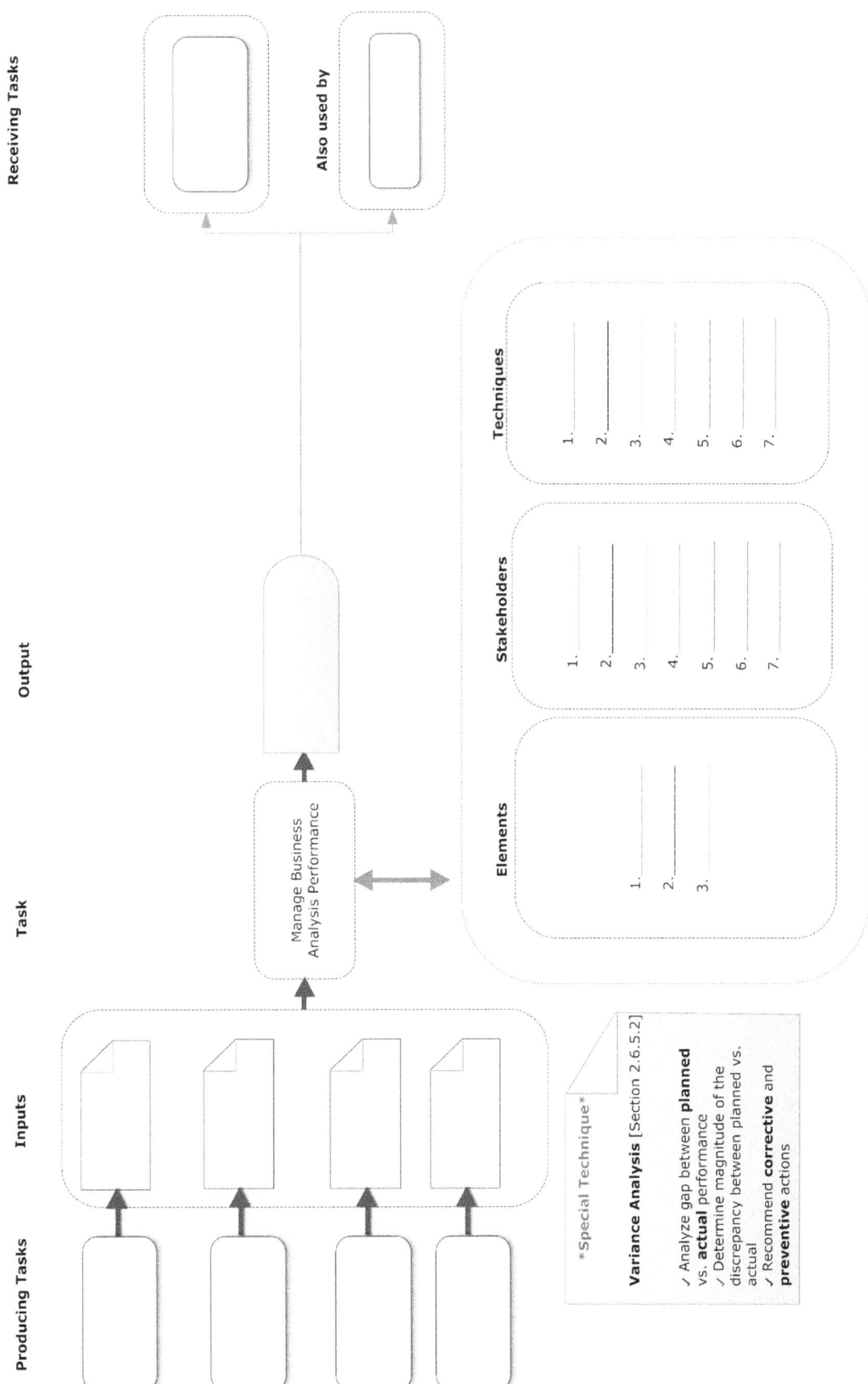

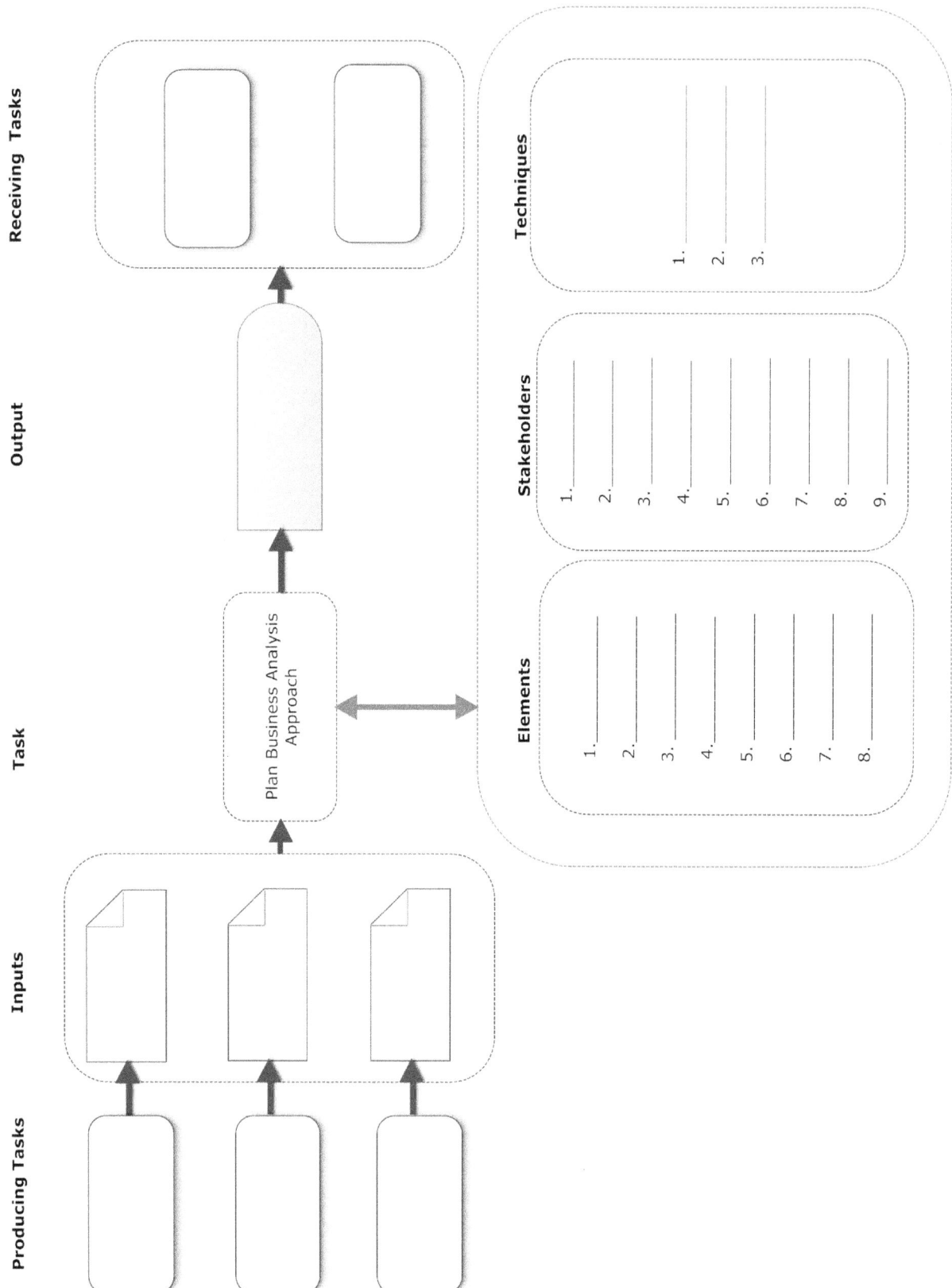

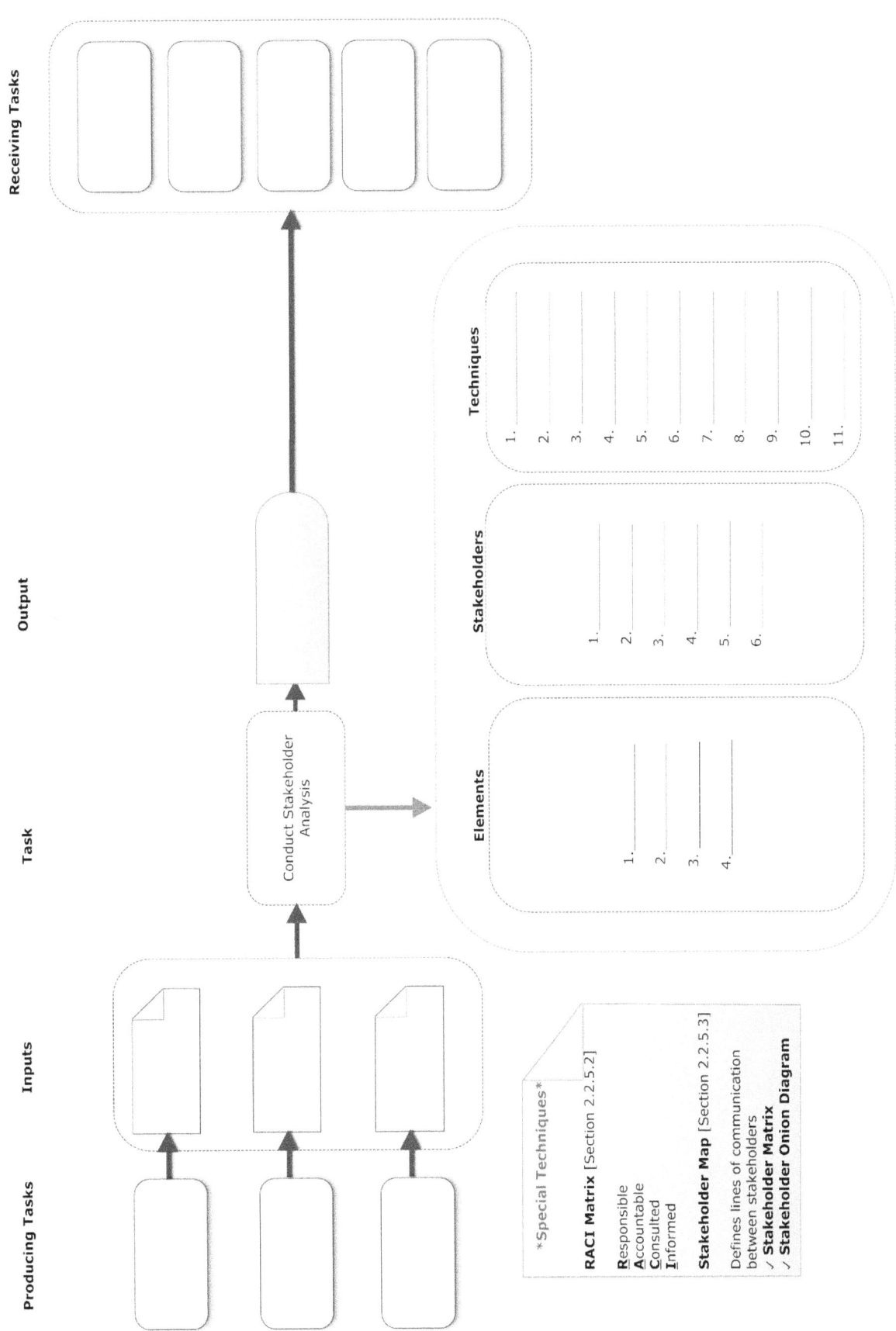

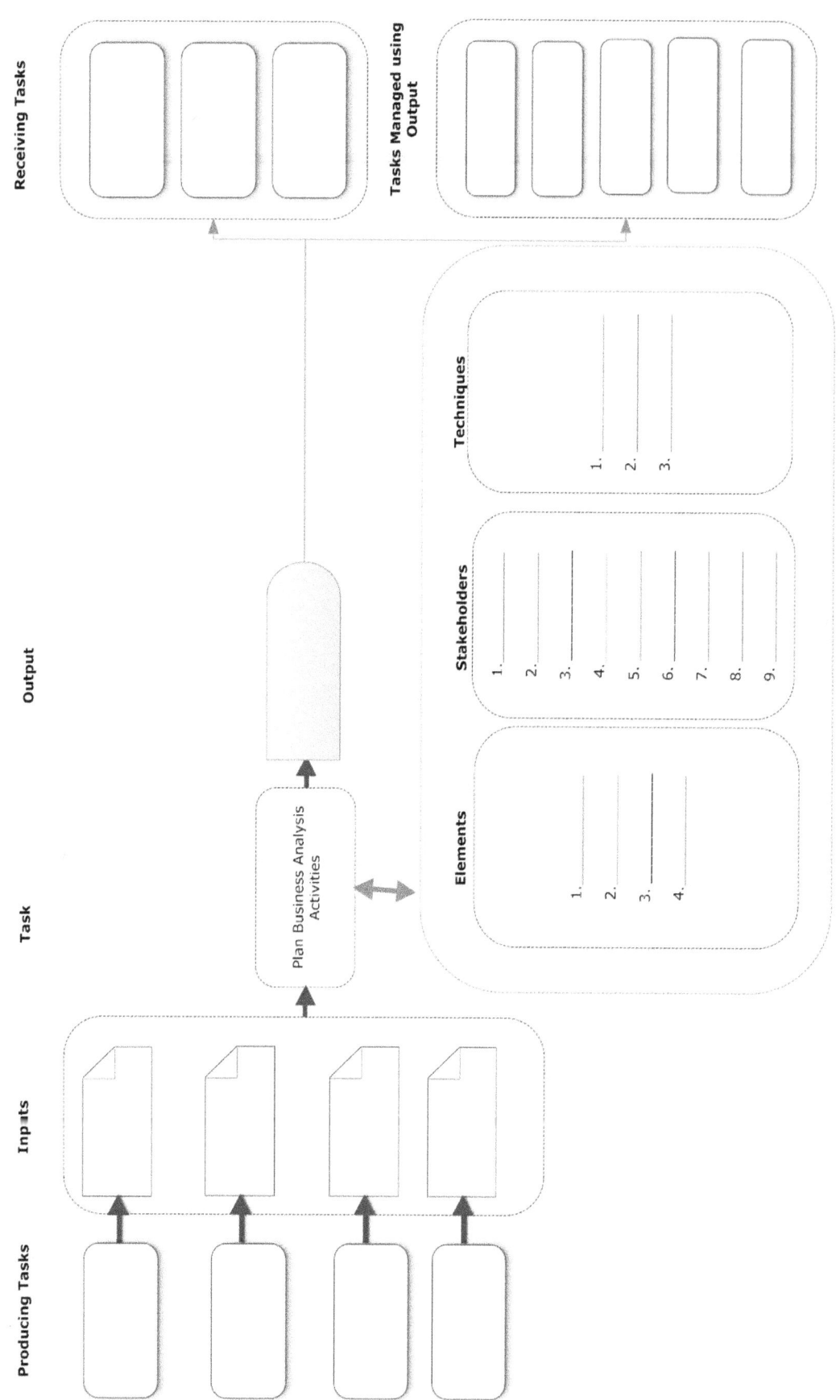

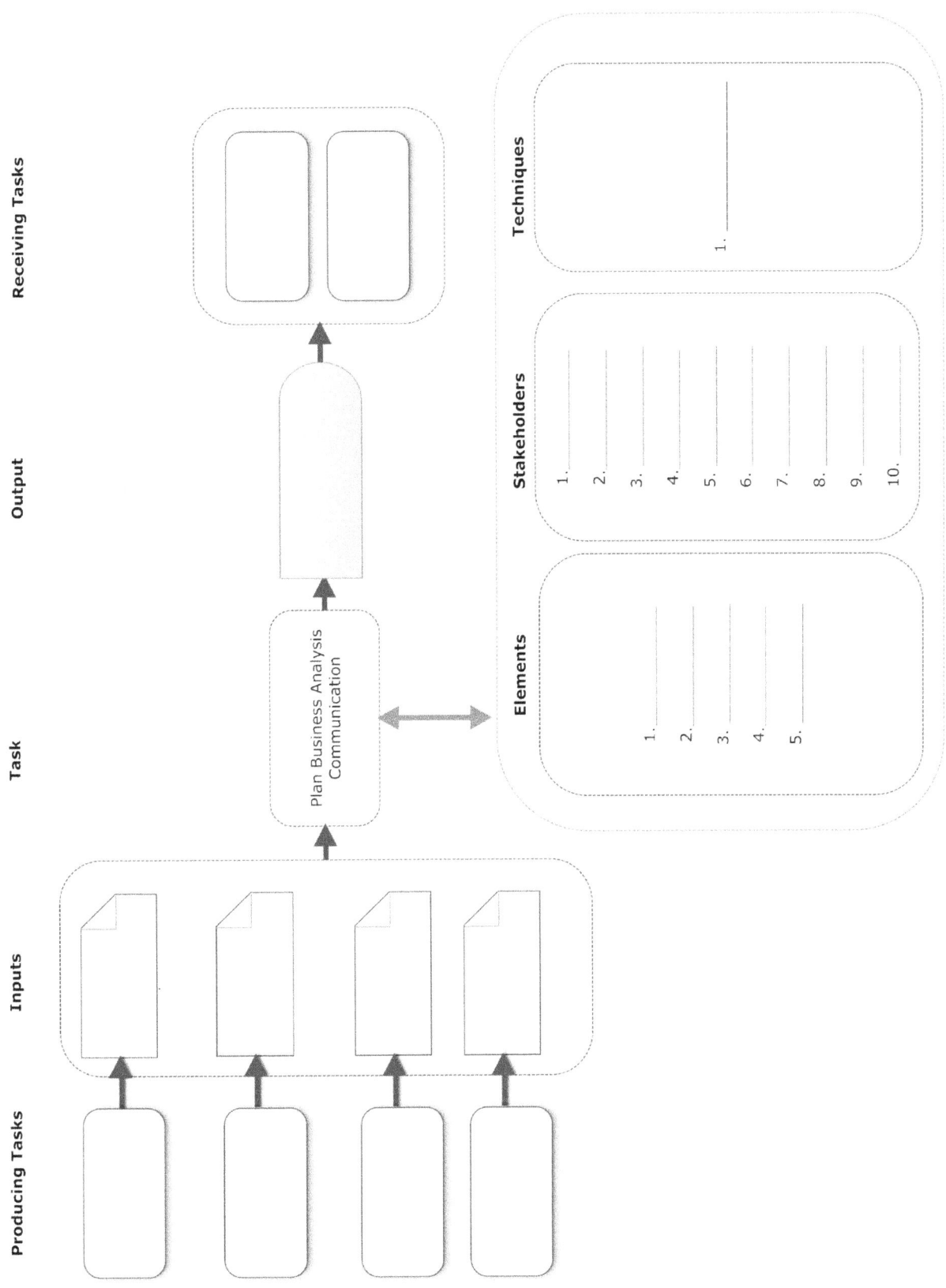

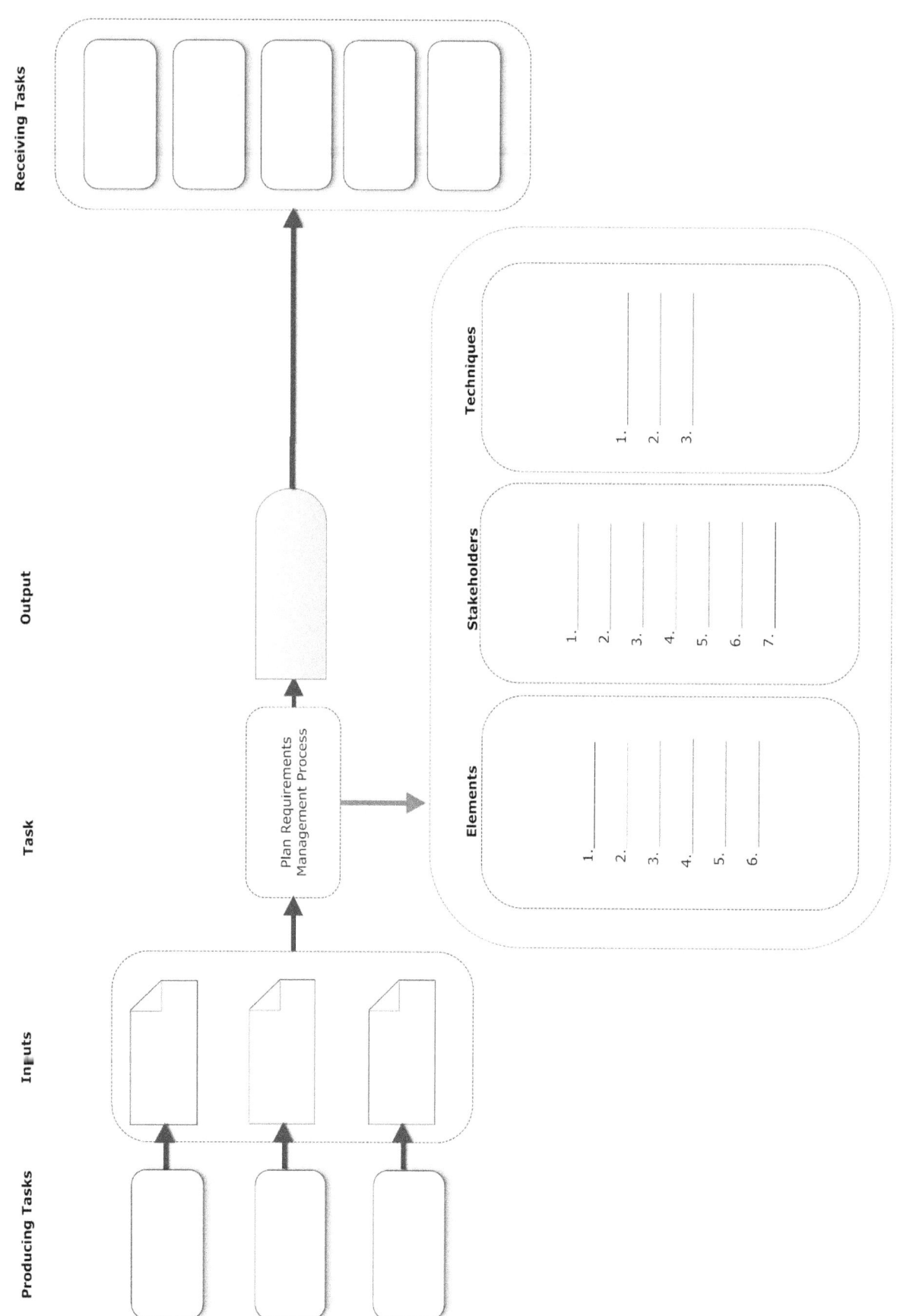

Chapter 3: Elicitation

Input/Tasks/Output Diagrams

(The order of diagram do not directly correspond to the order of tasks as listed in the BABOK®)

Inputs

Tasks

Outputs

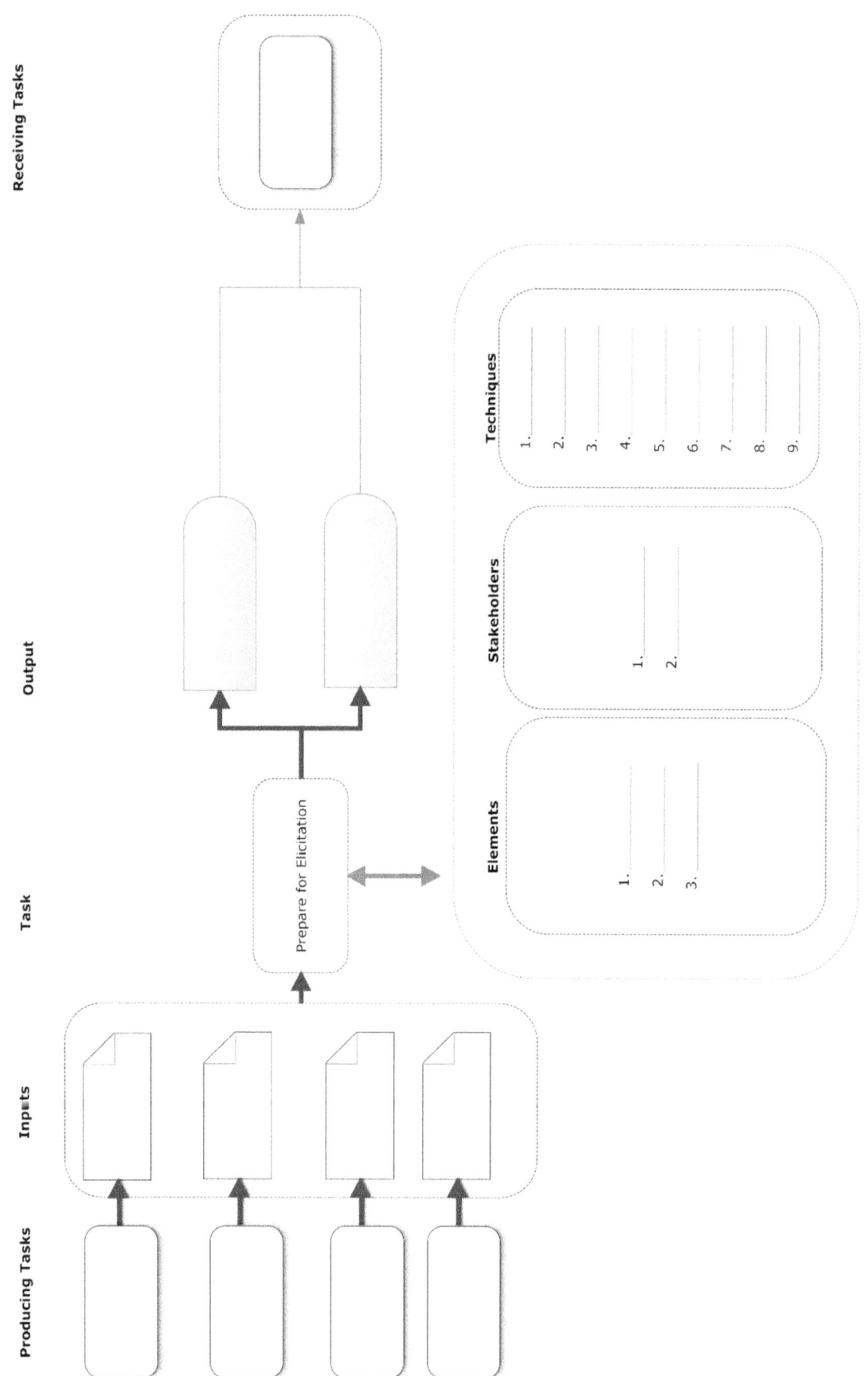

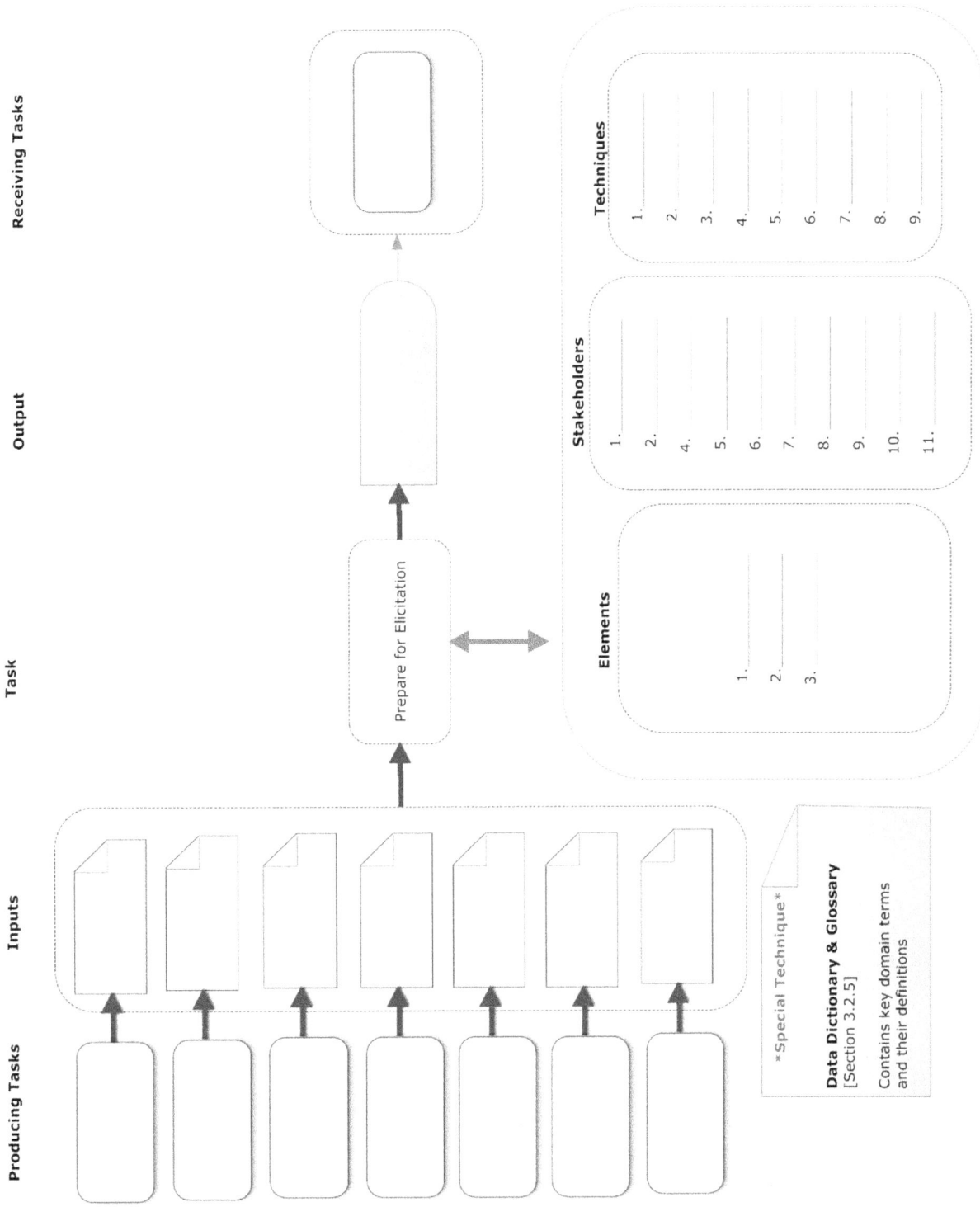

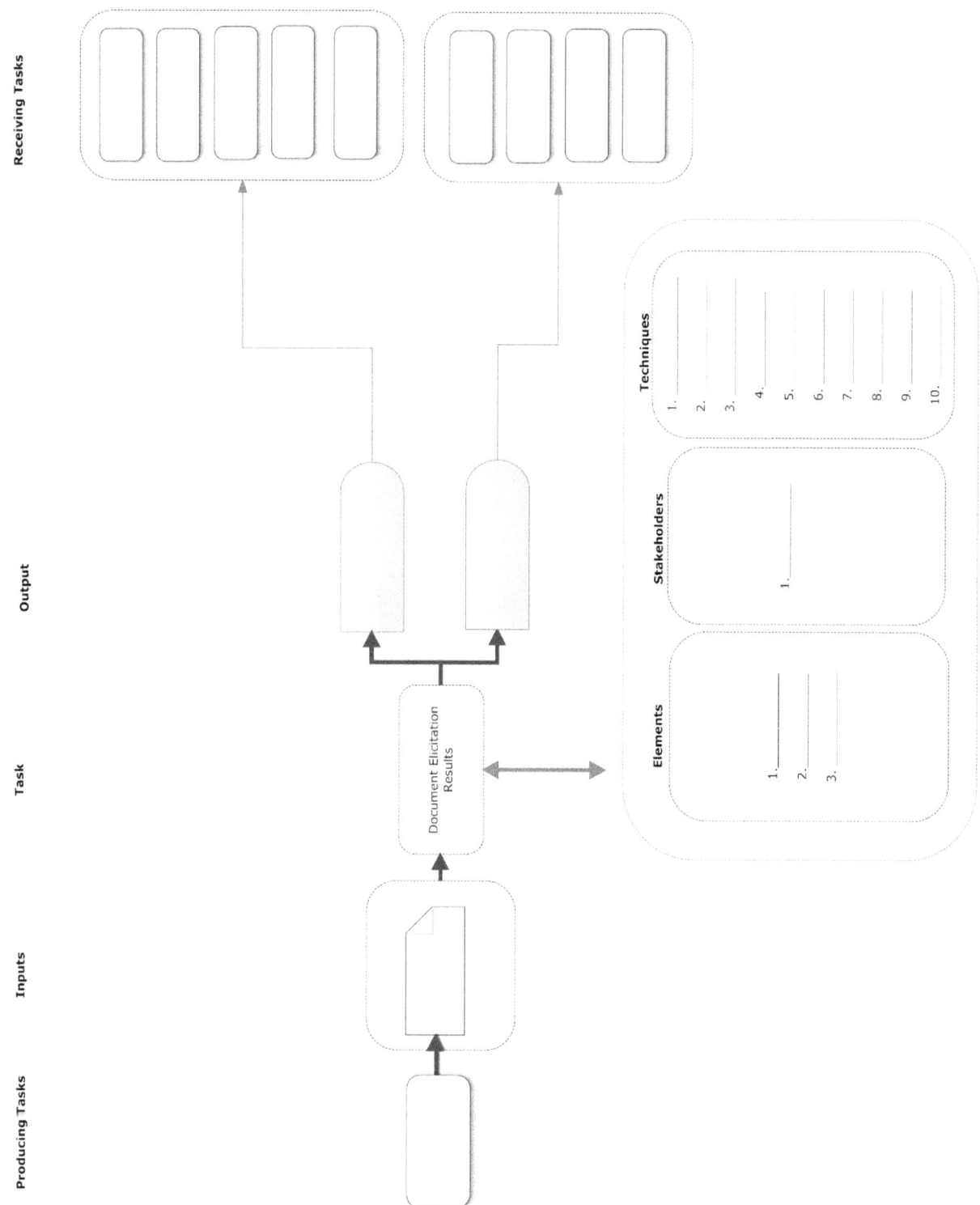

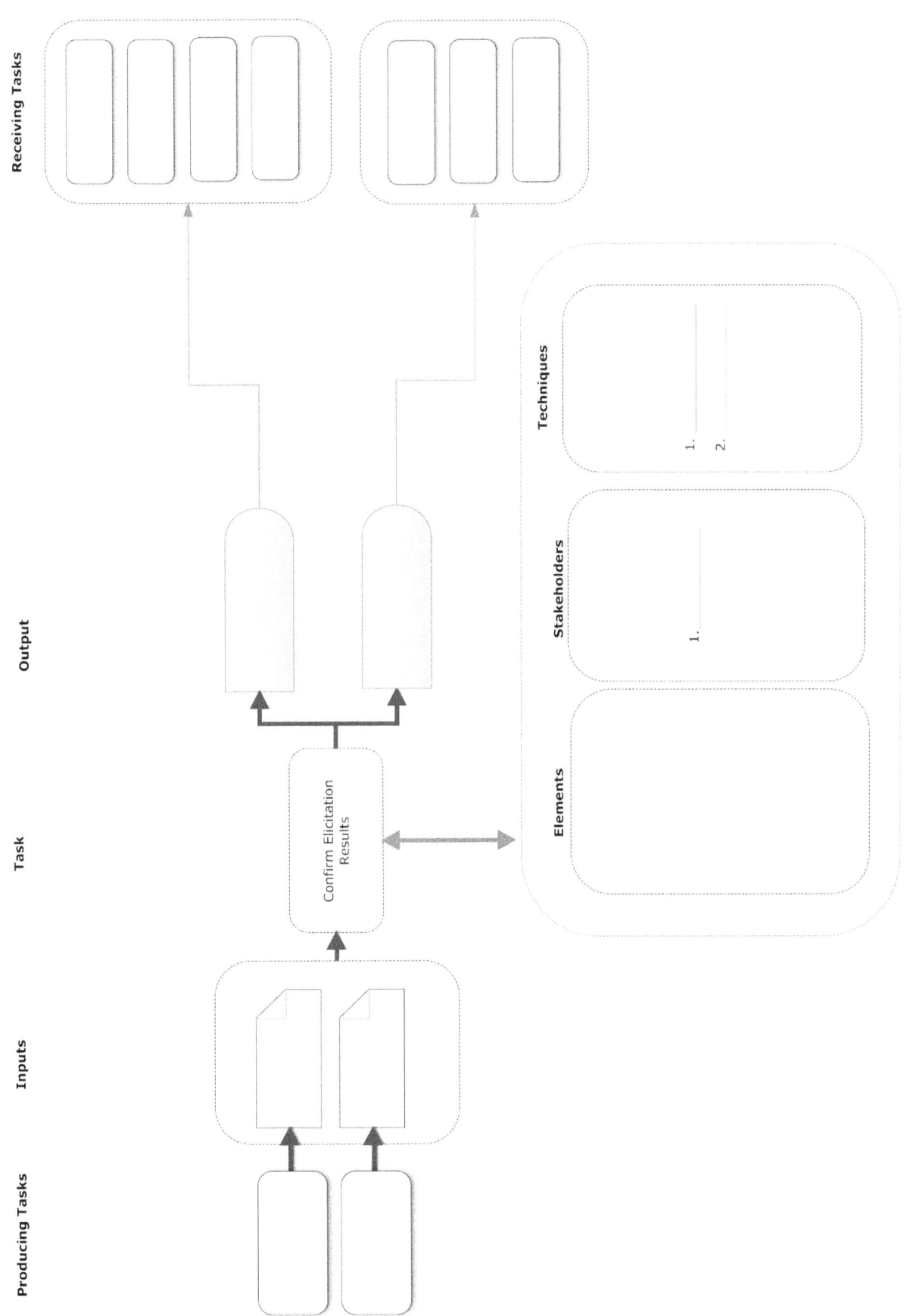

Chapter 4: Requirements Management & Communication

Input/Tasks/Output Diagrams

(The order of diagrams do not directly correspond to the order of tasks as listed in the BABOK®)

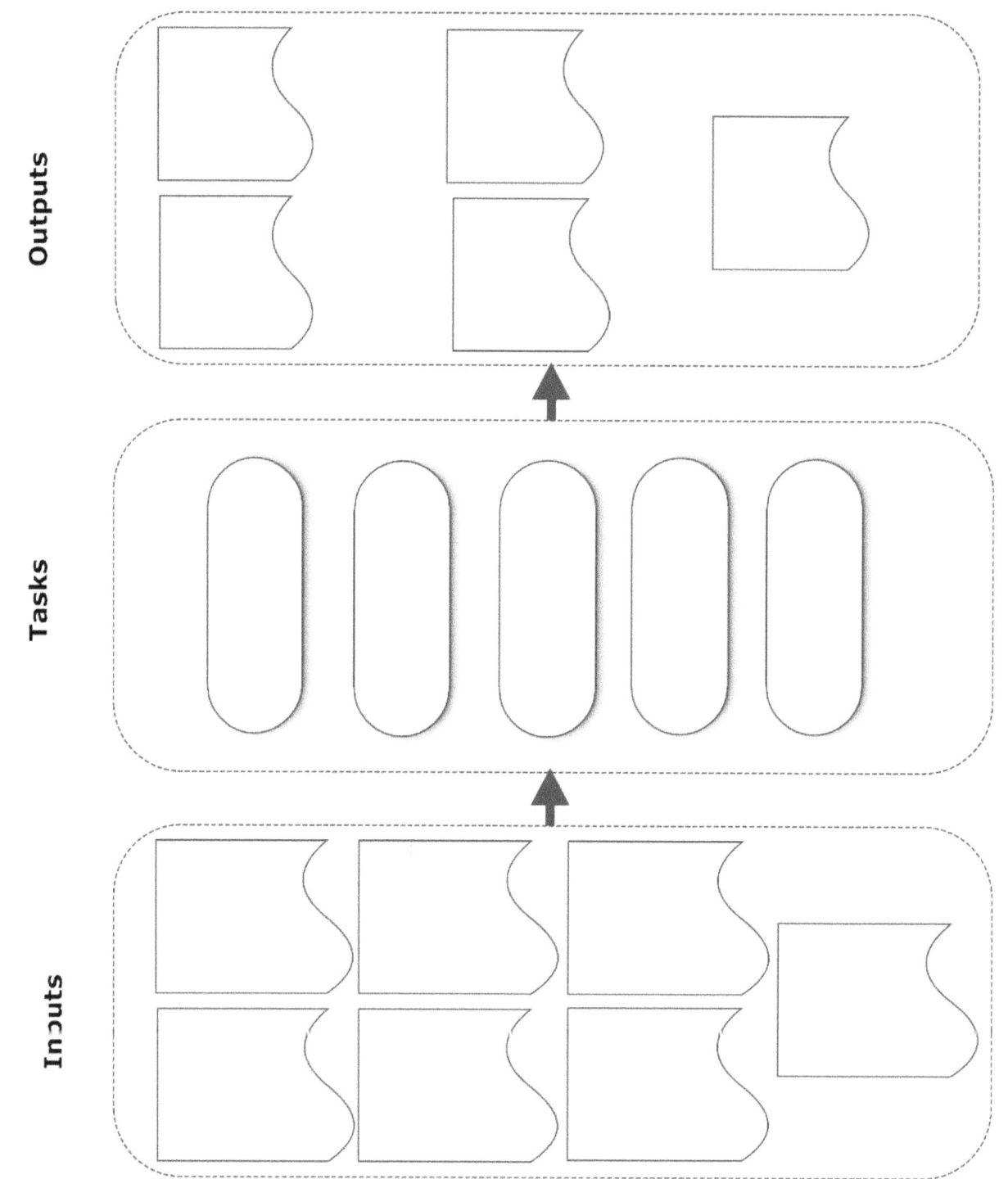

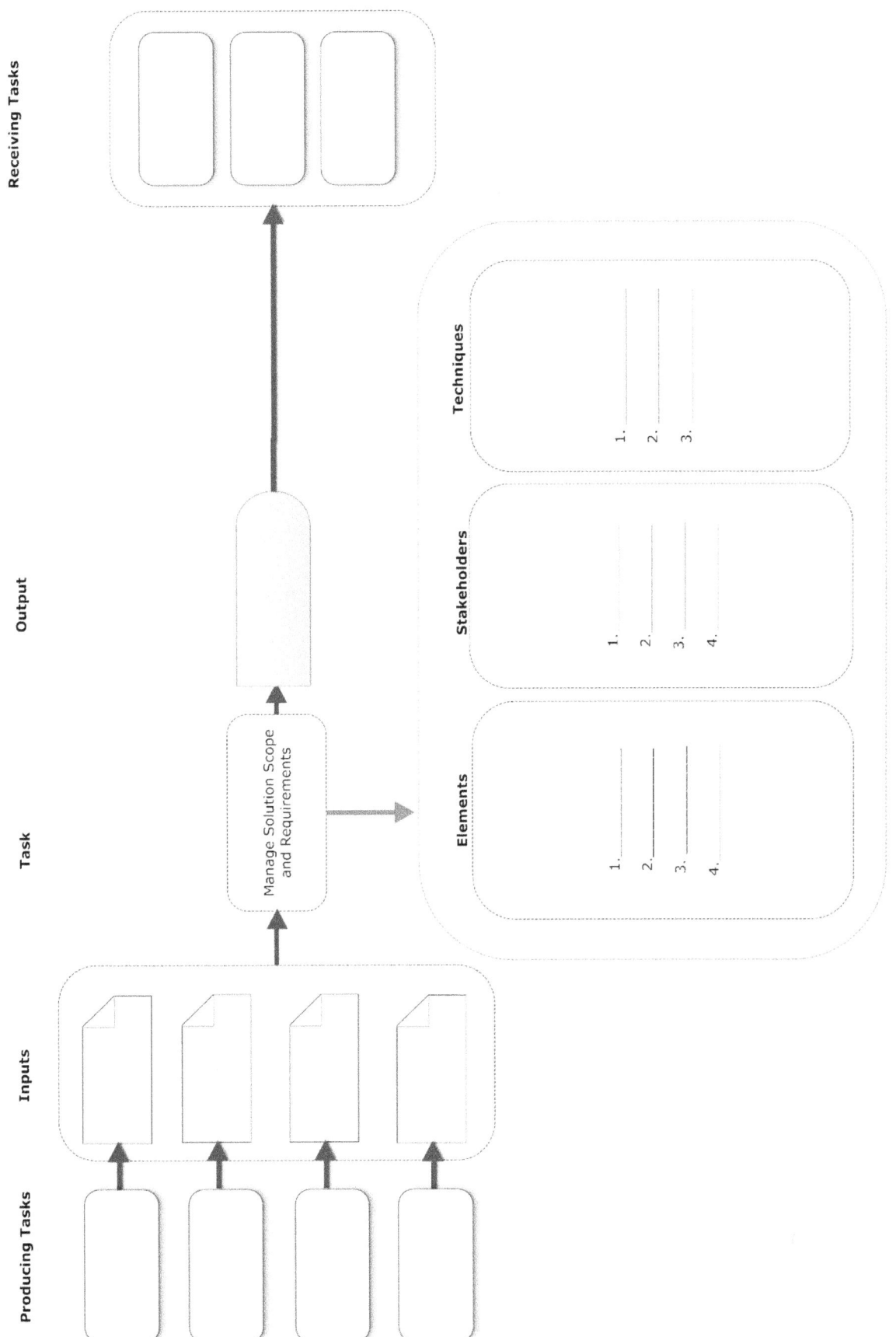

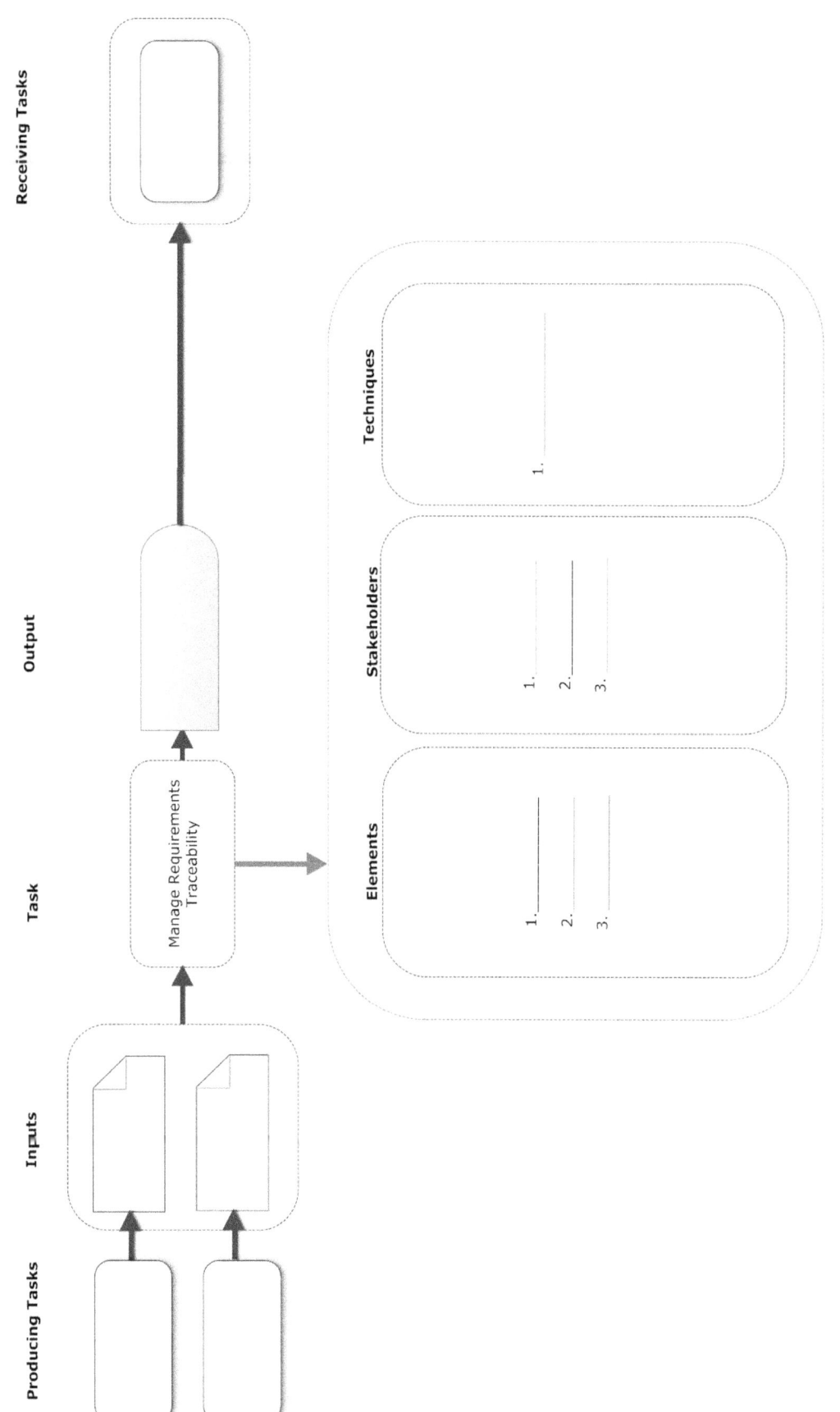

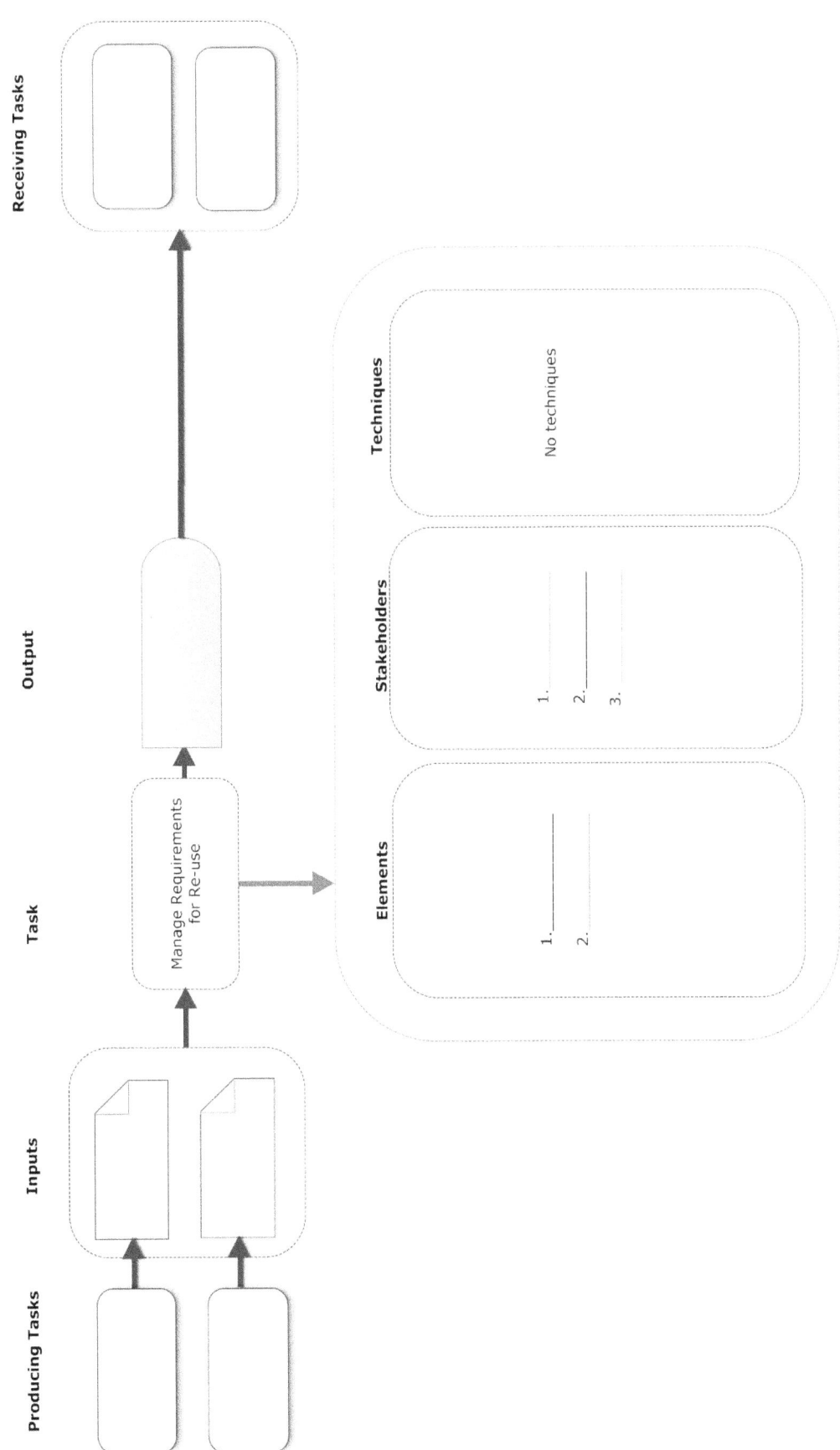

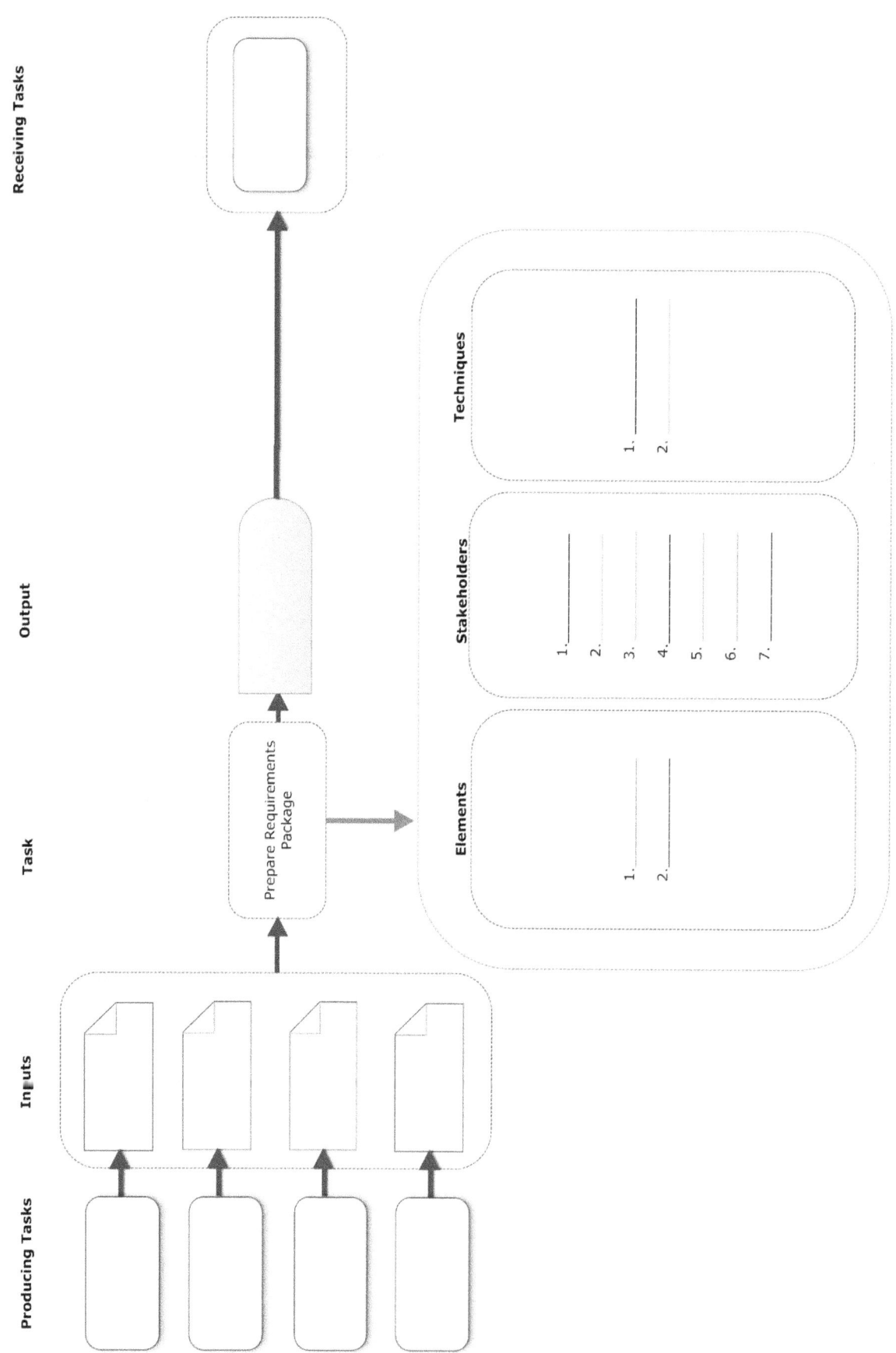

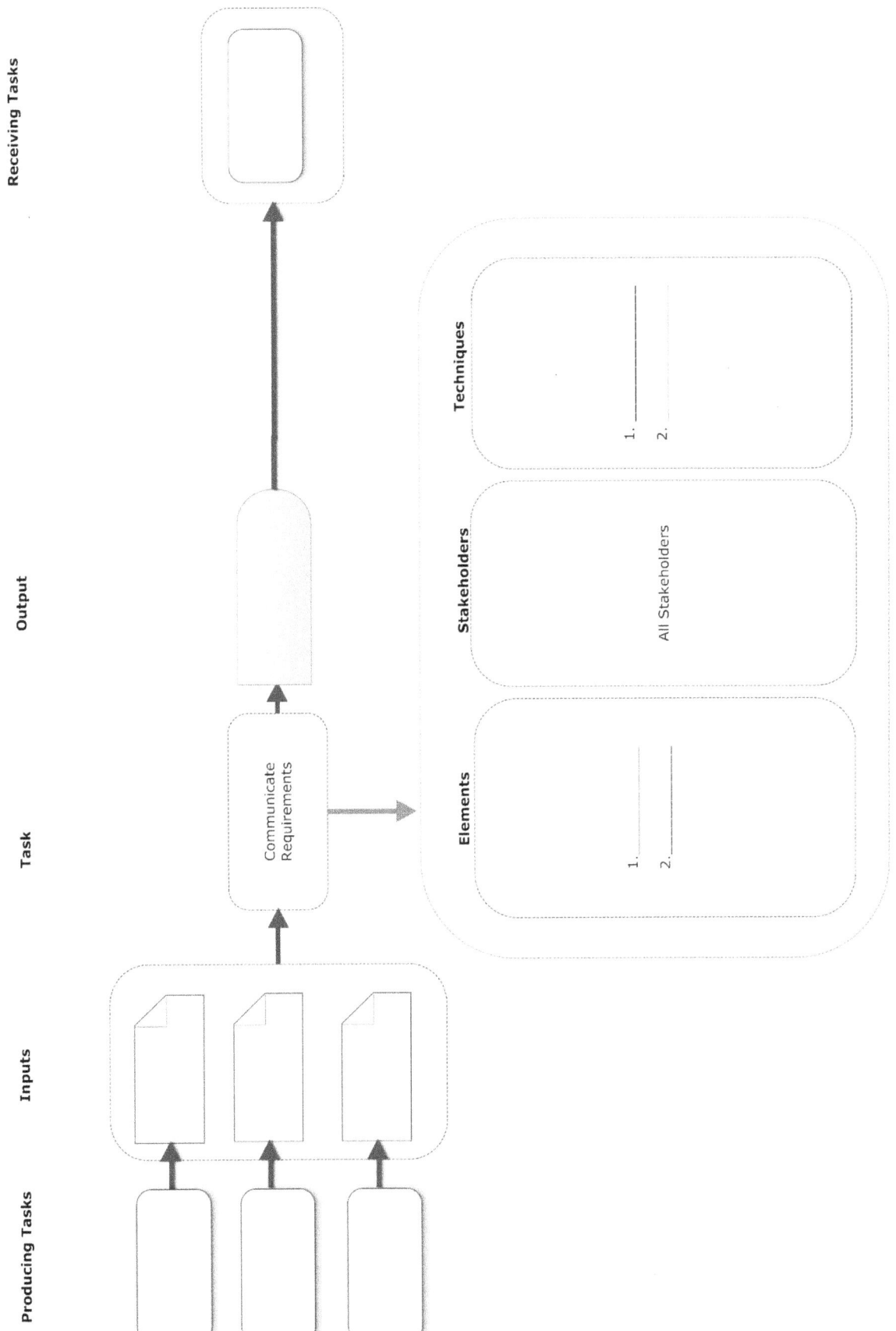

Chapter 5: Enterprise Analysis
Input/Tasks/Output Diagrams
(The order of diagram do not directly correspond to the order of tasks as listed in the BABOK®)

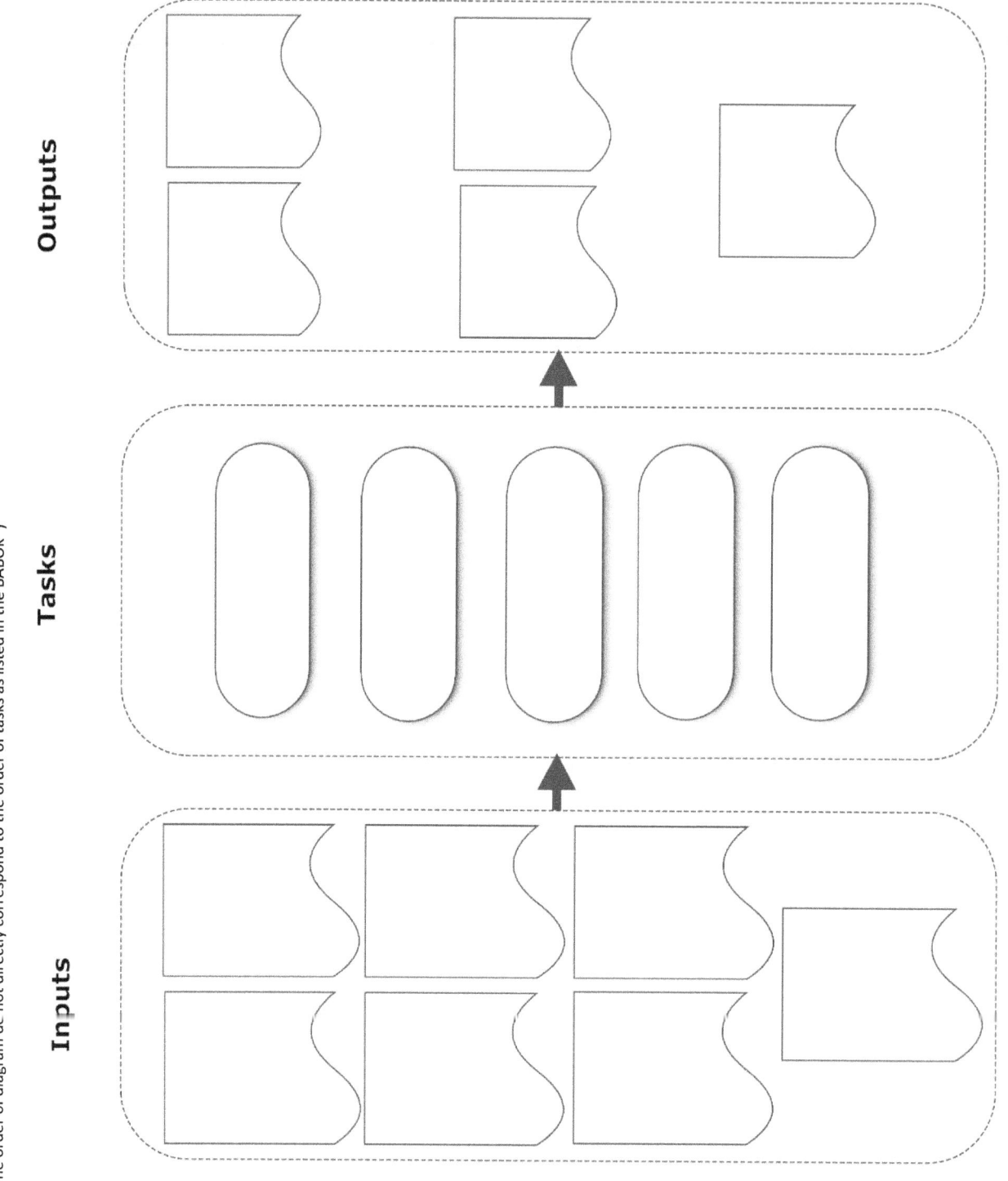

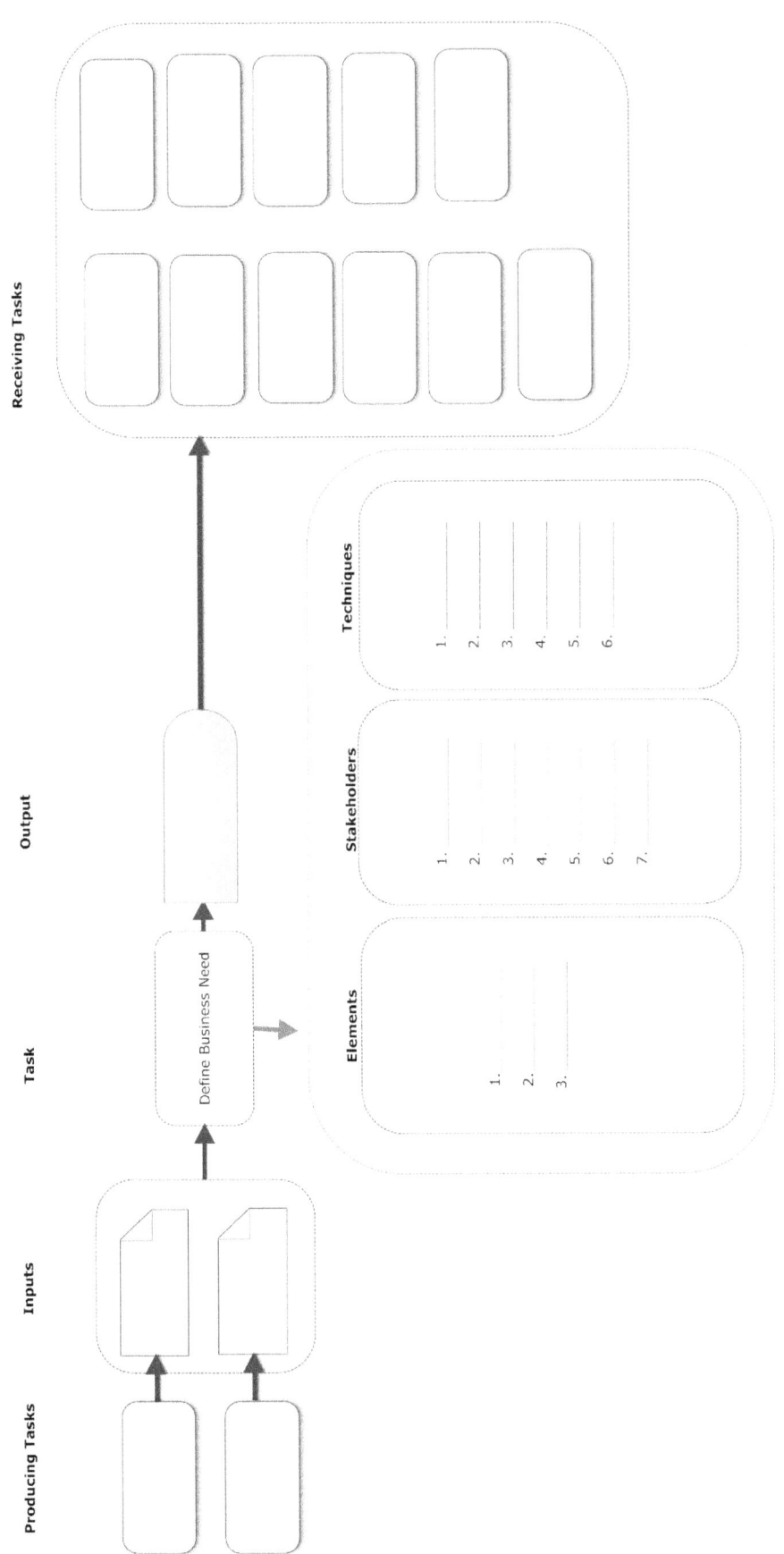

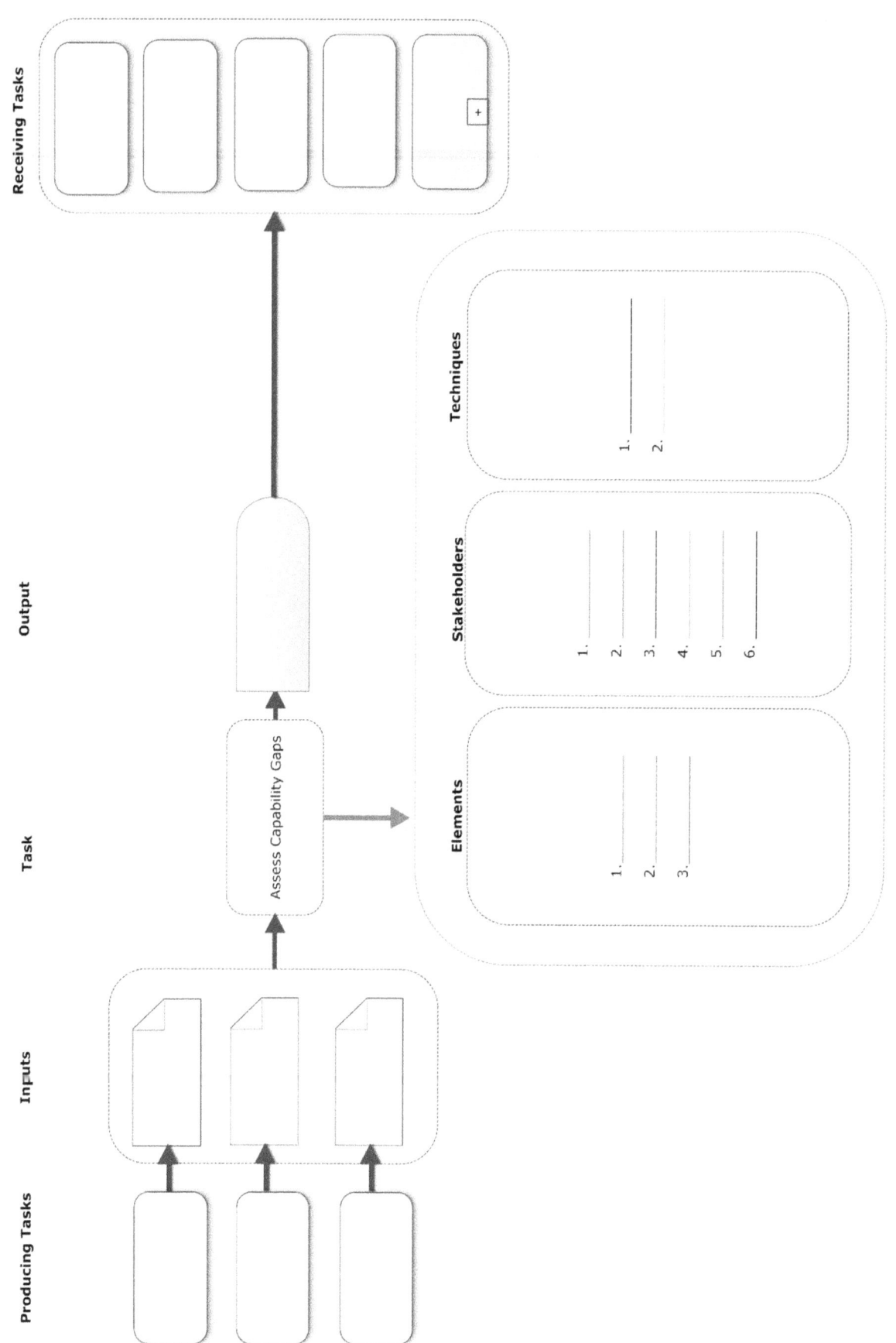

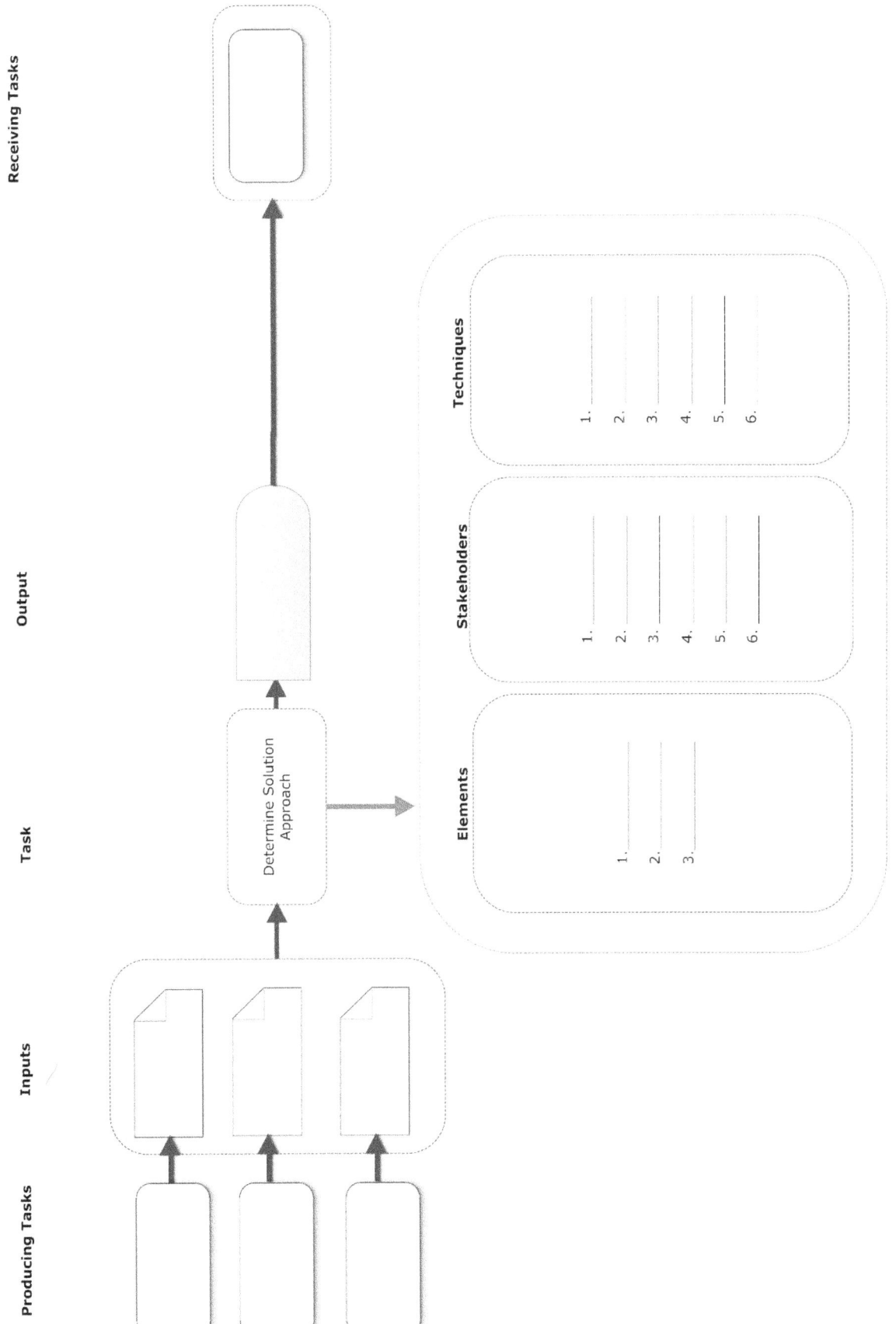

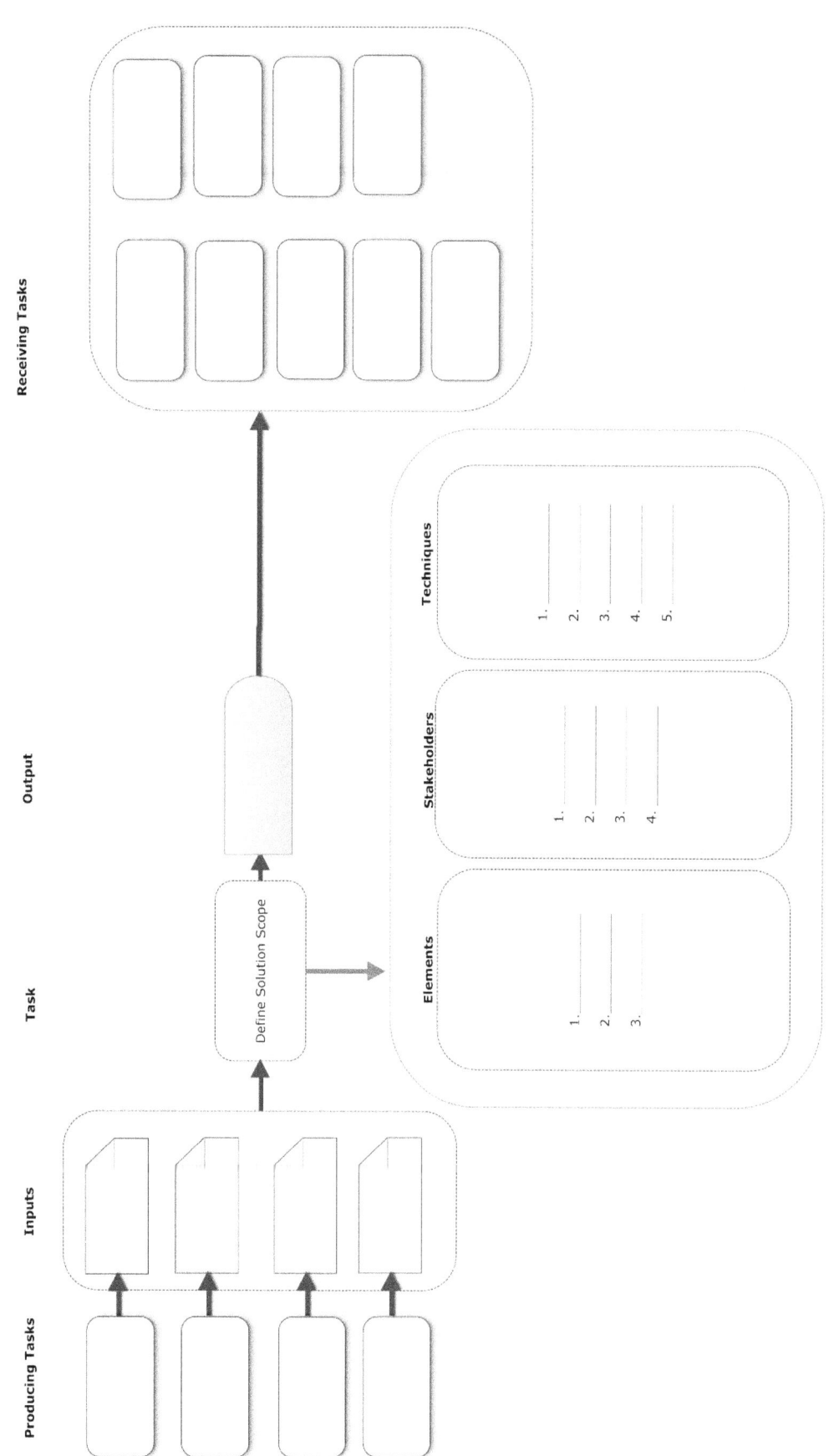

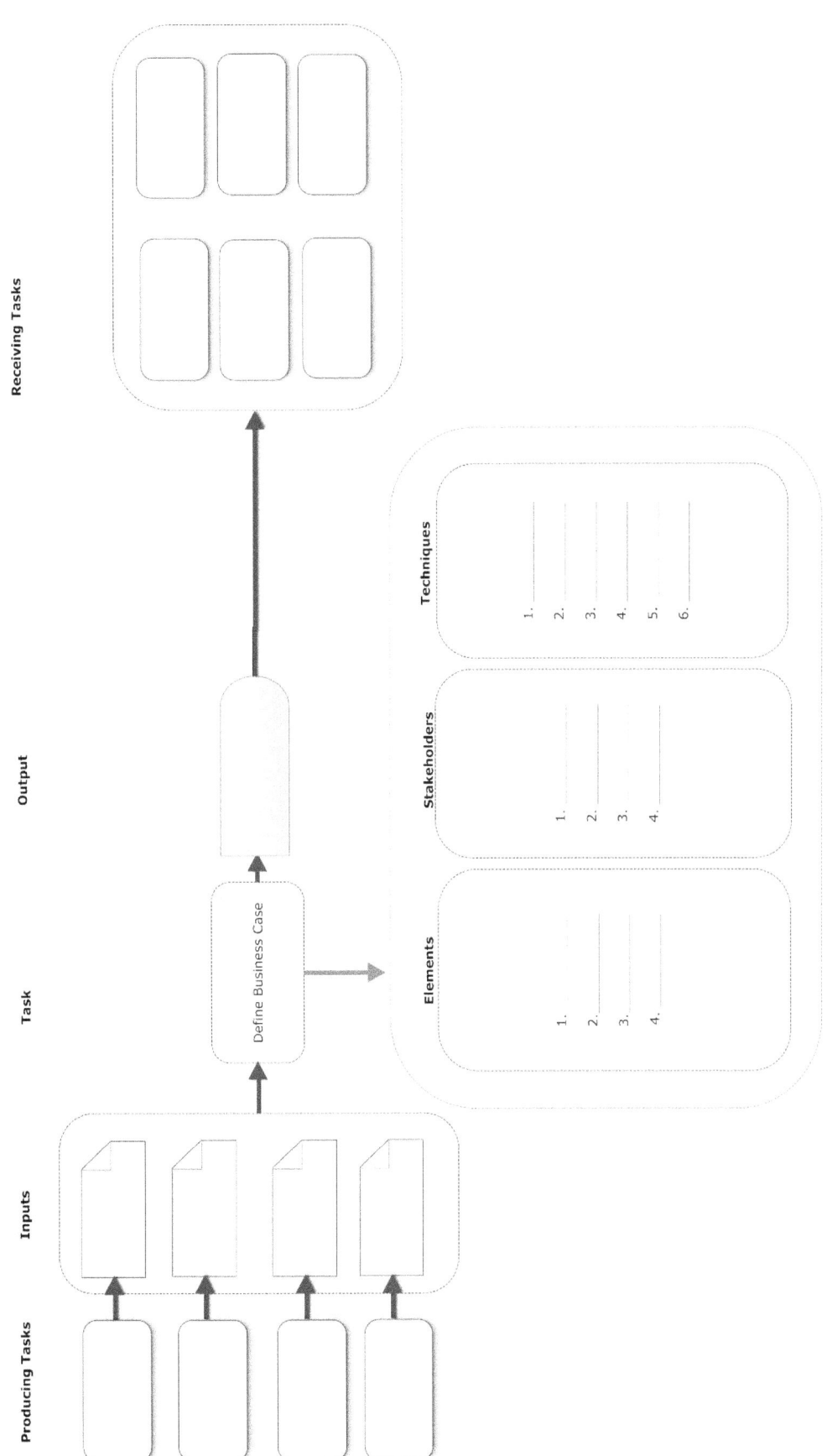

Chapter 6: Requirement Analysis
Input/Tasks/Output Diagrams
(The order of diagram do not directly correspond to the order of tasks as listed in the BABOK®)

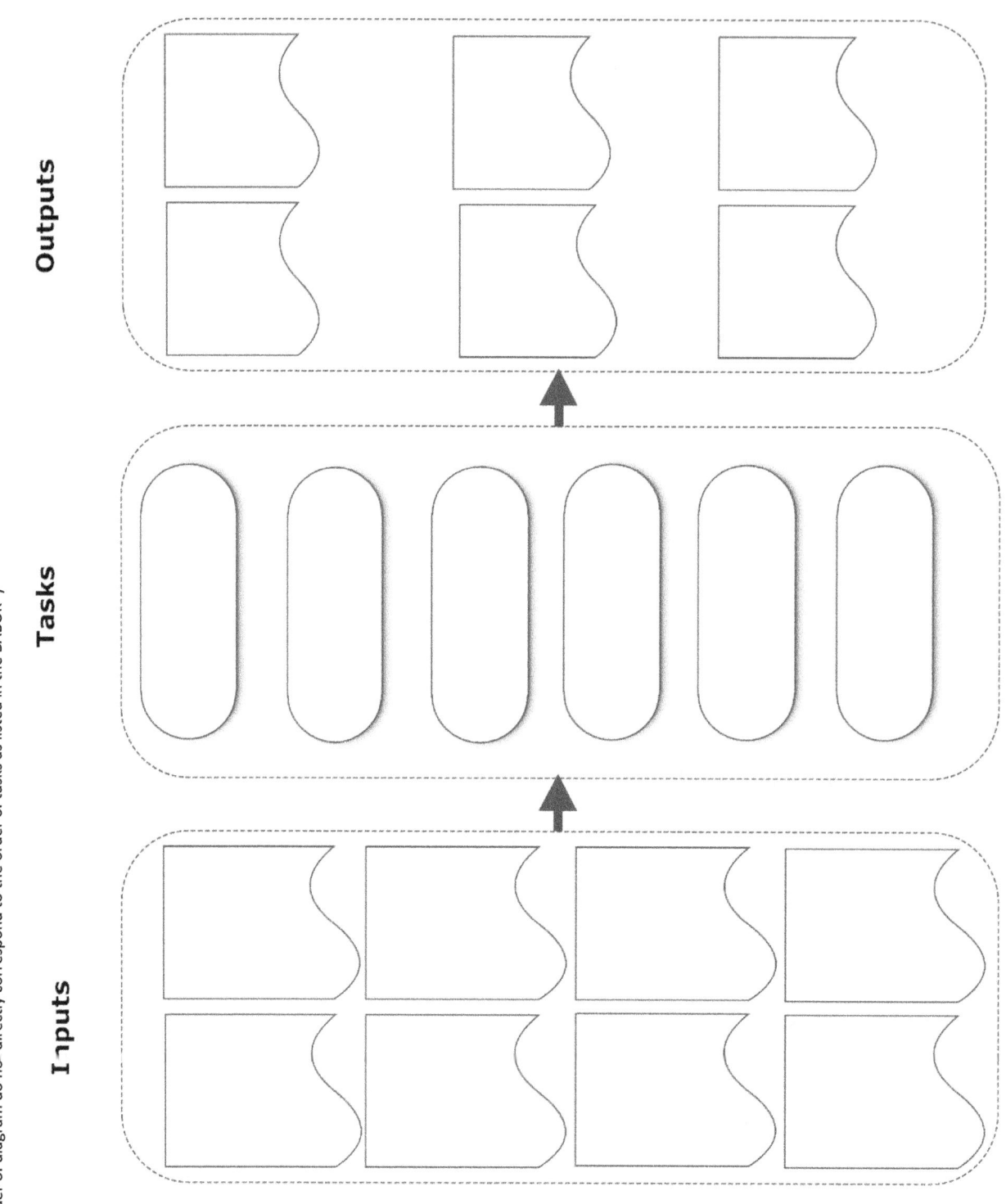

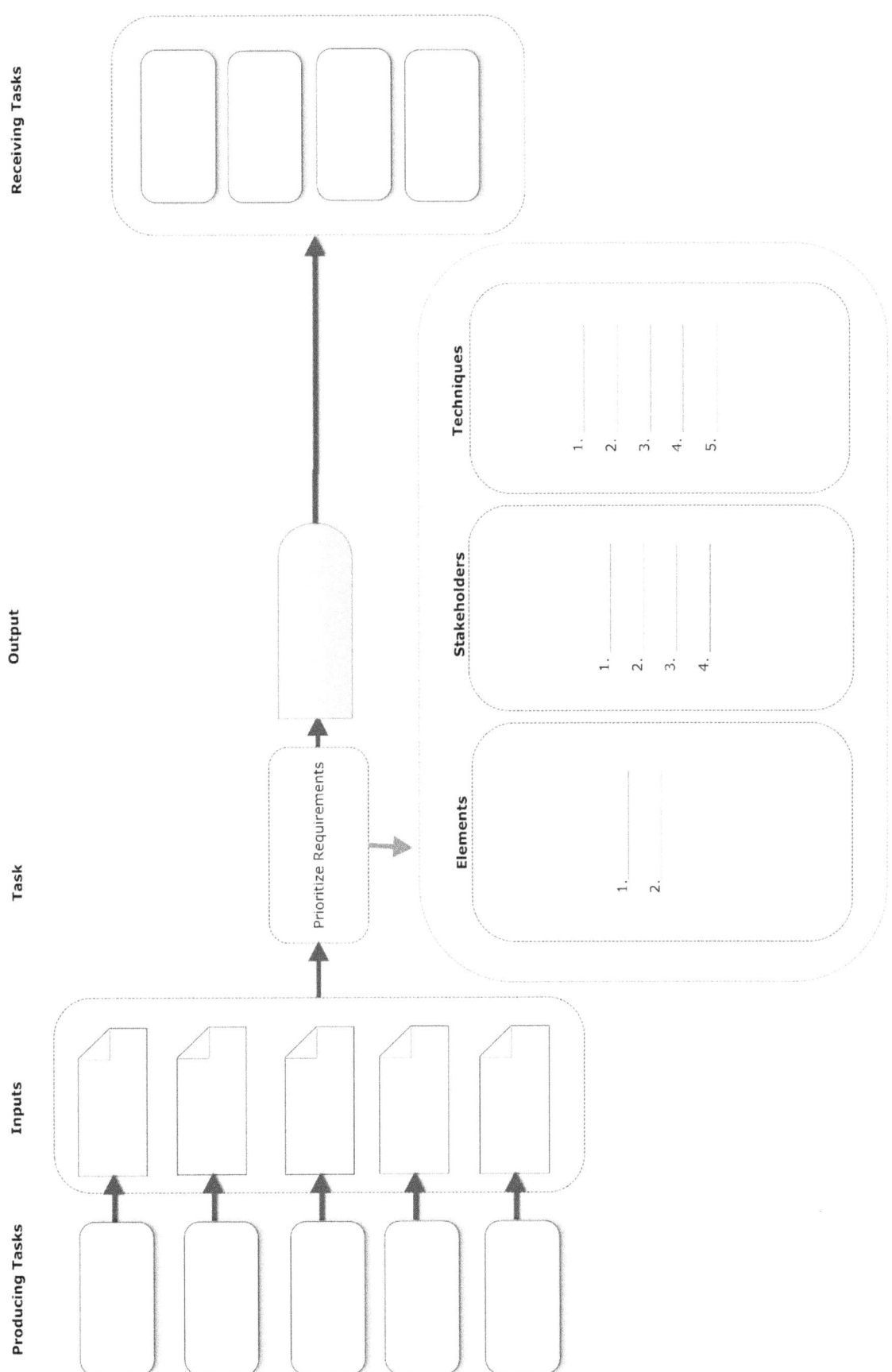

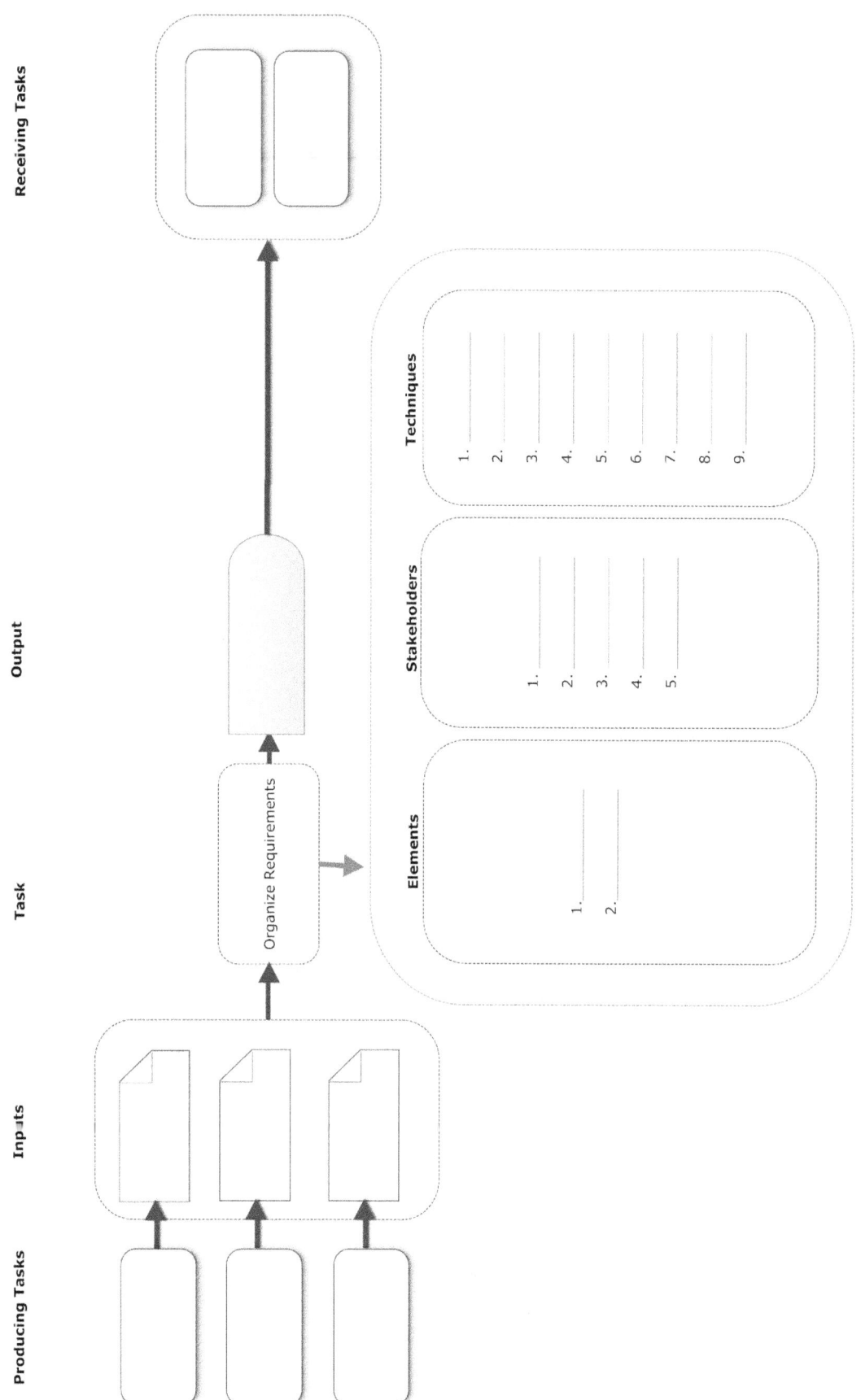

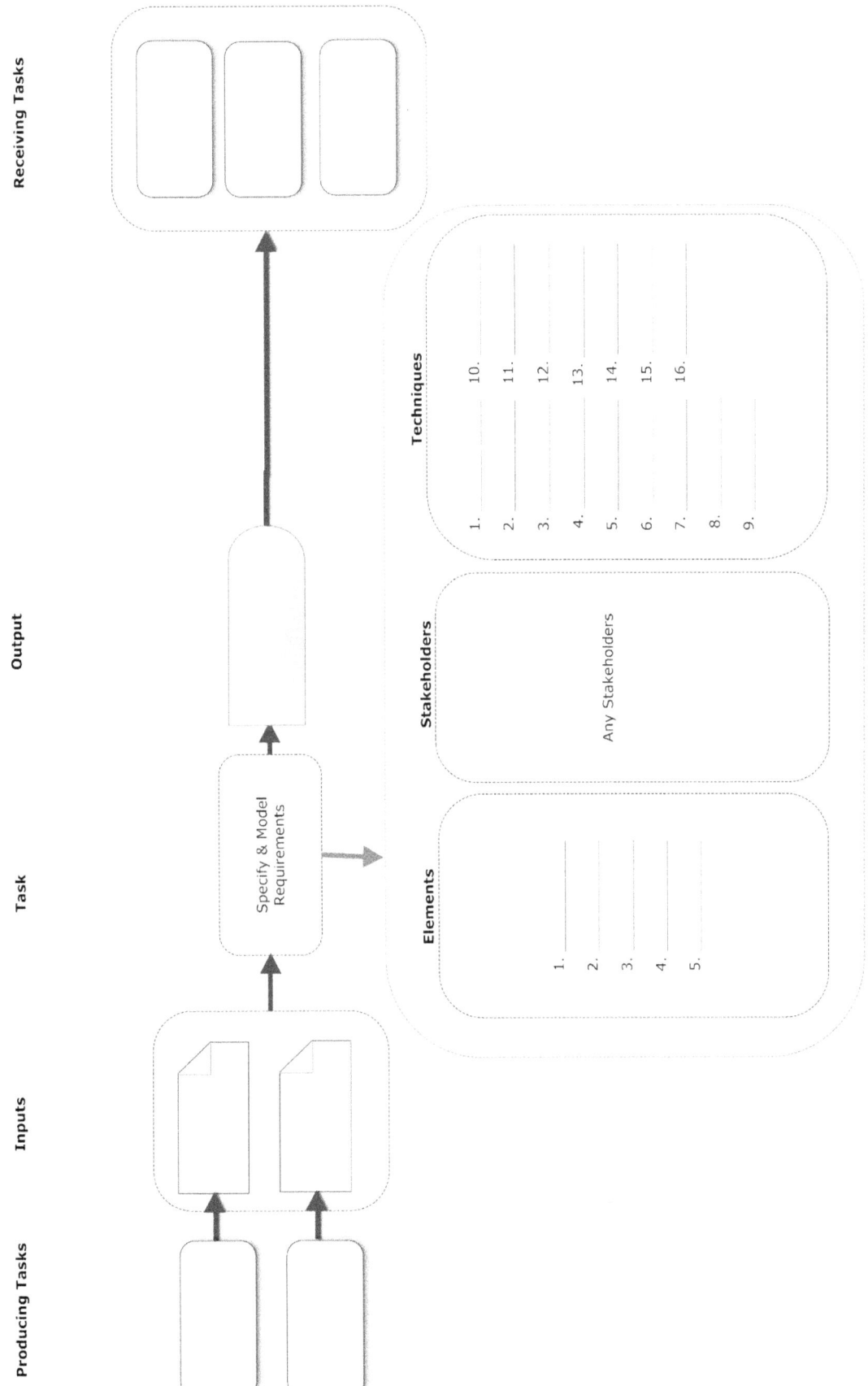

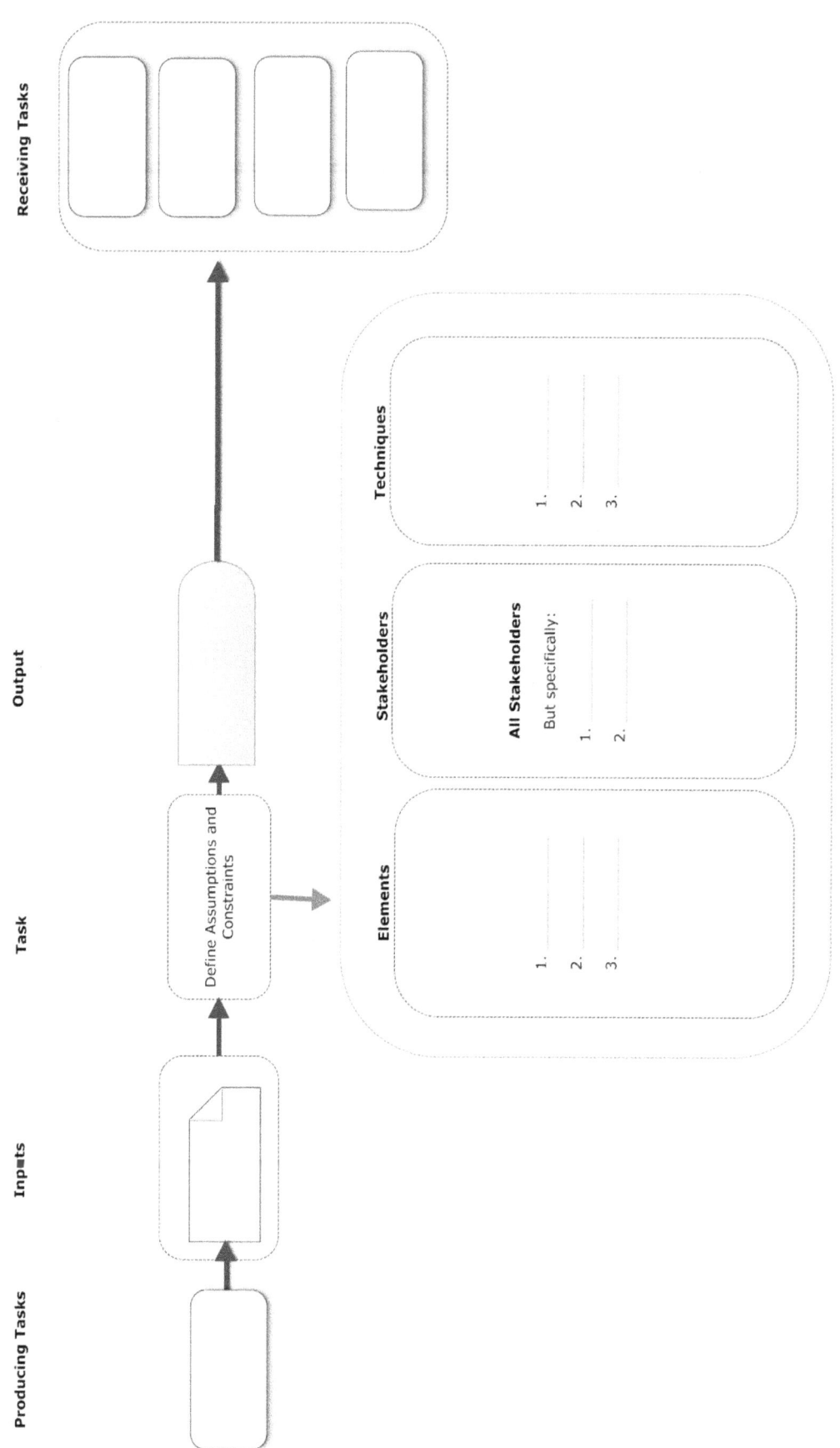

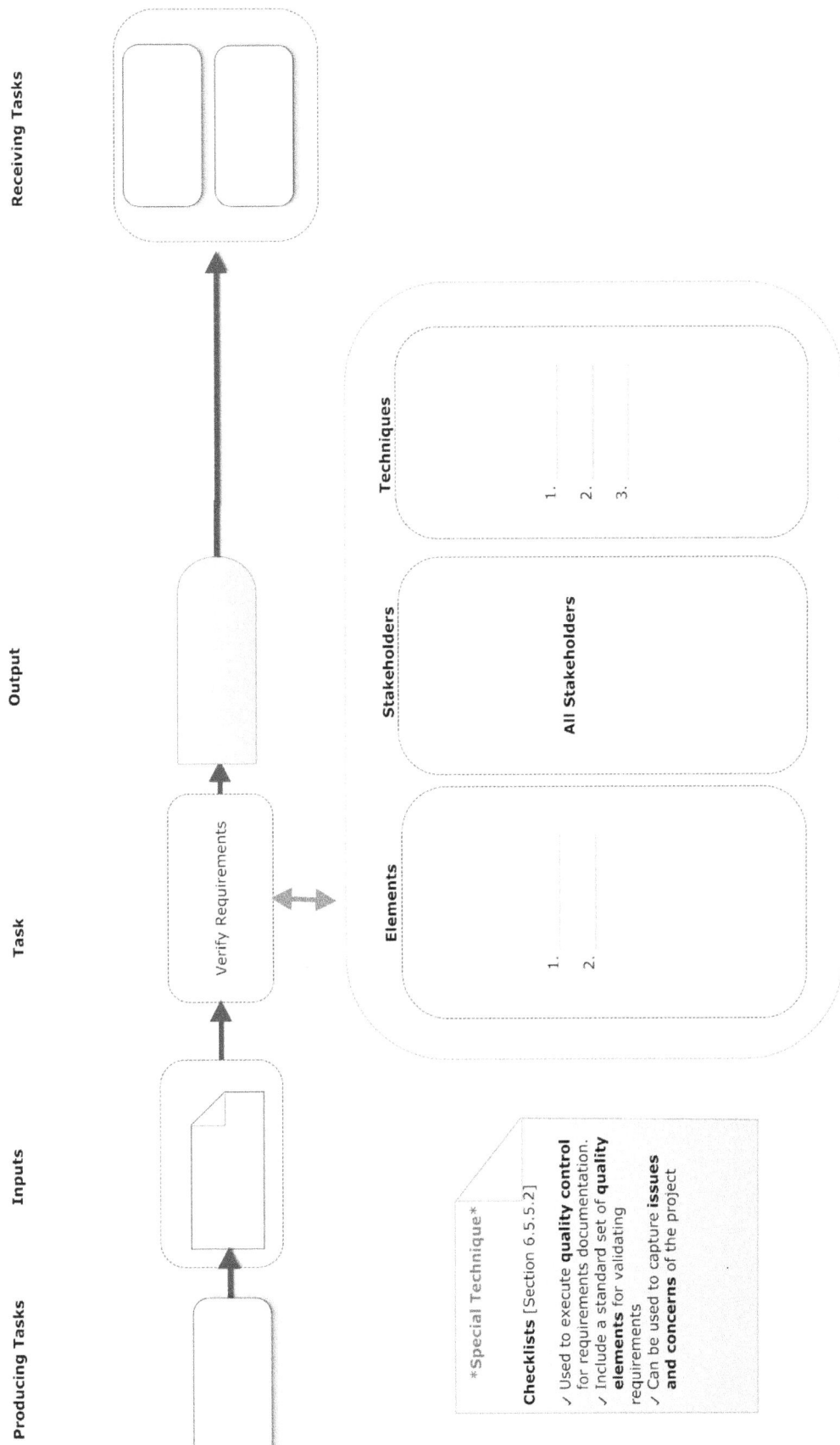

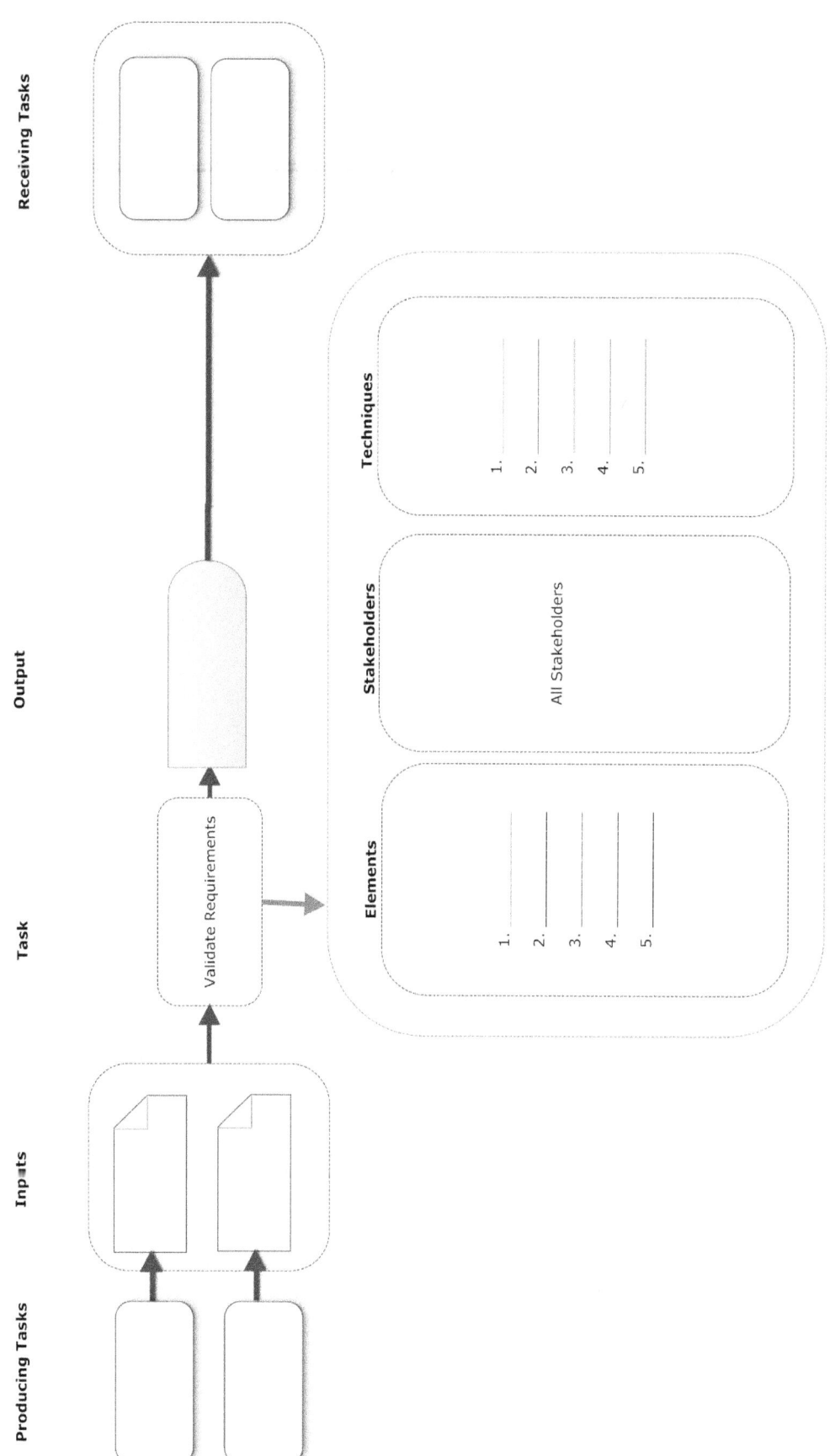

Chapter 7 : Solution Assessment & Validation

Input/Tasks/Output Diagrams

(The order of diagram do not directly correspond to the order of tasks as listed in the BABOK®)

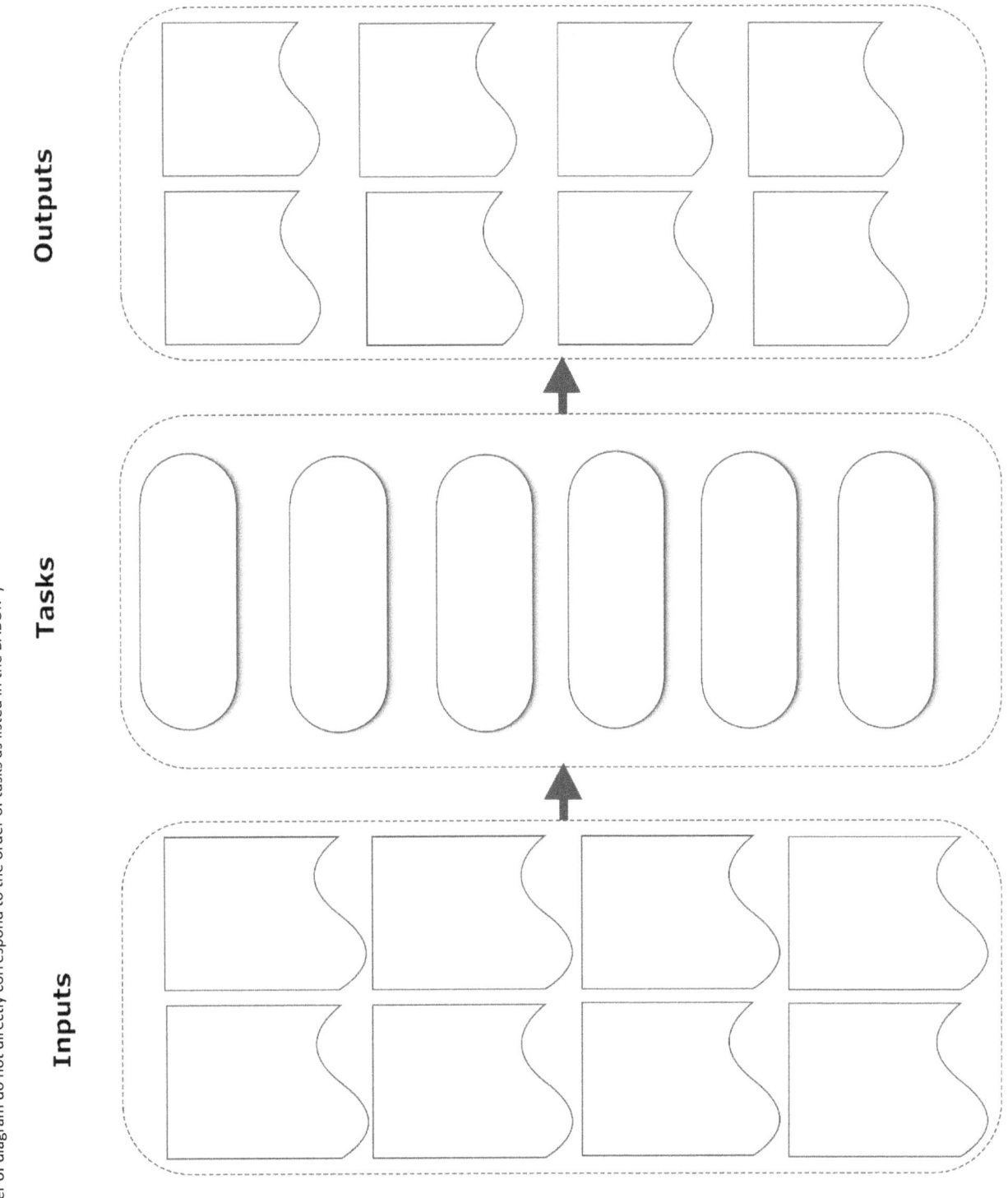

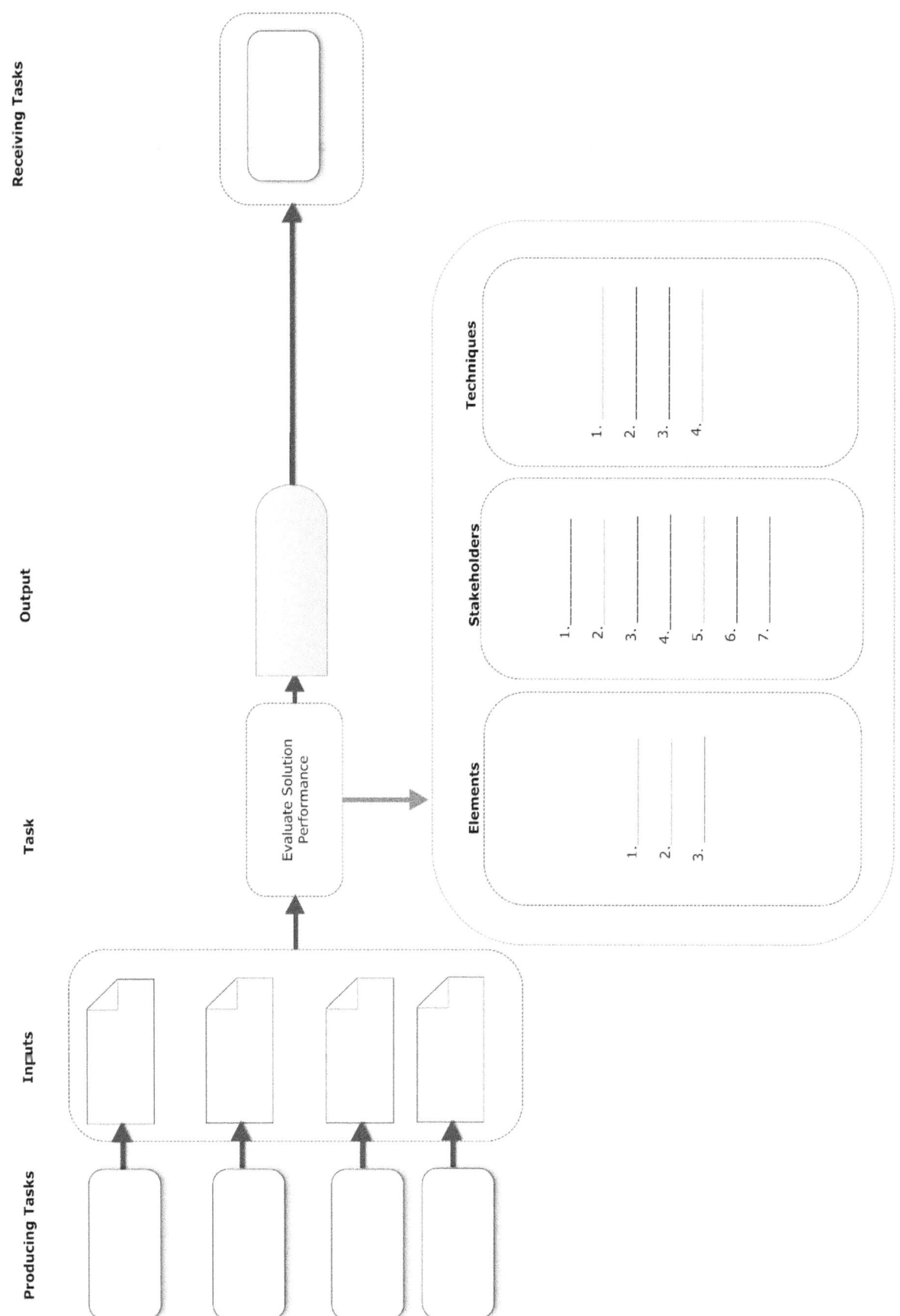

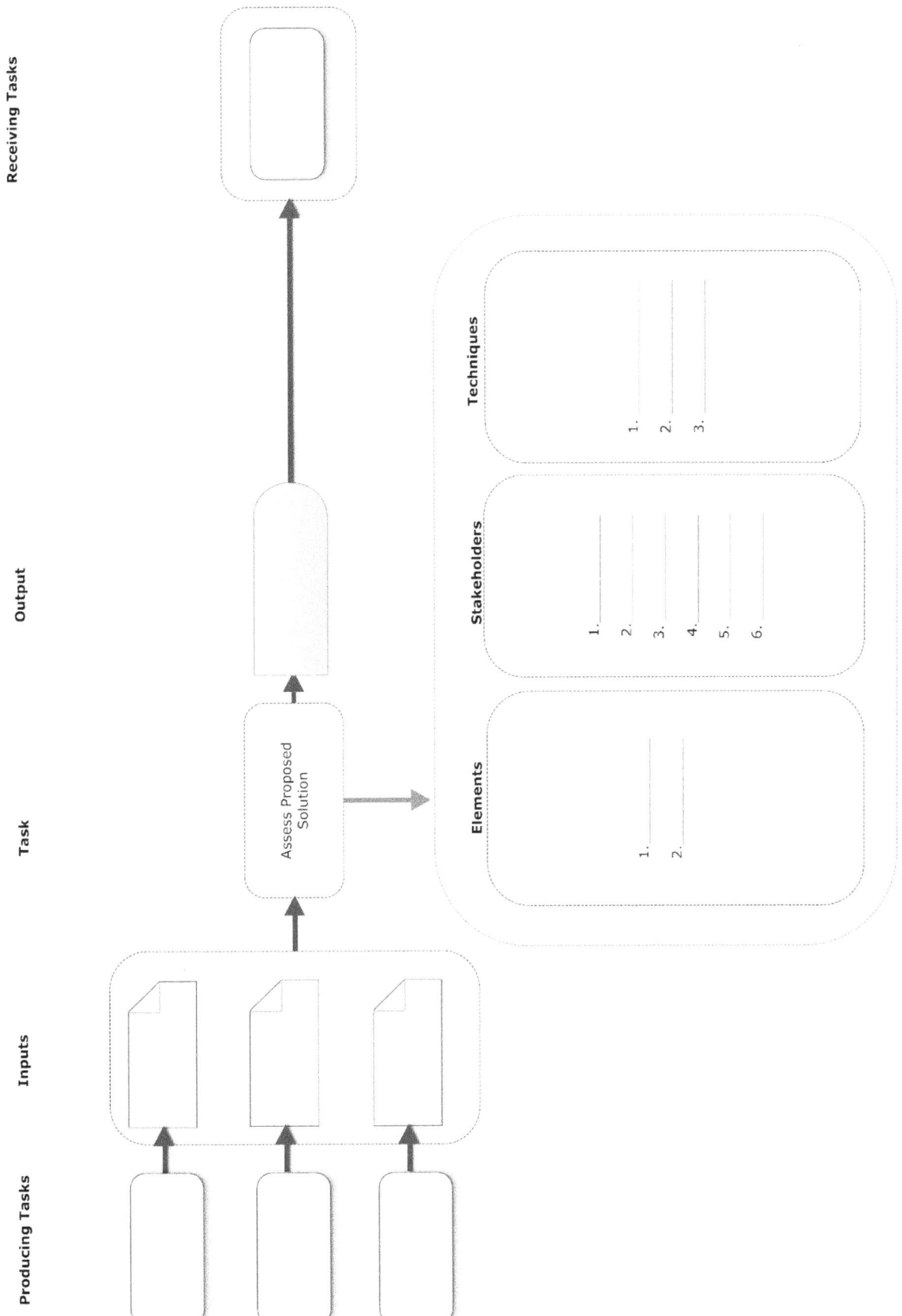

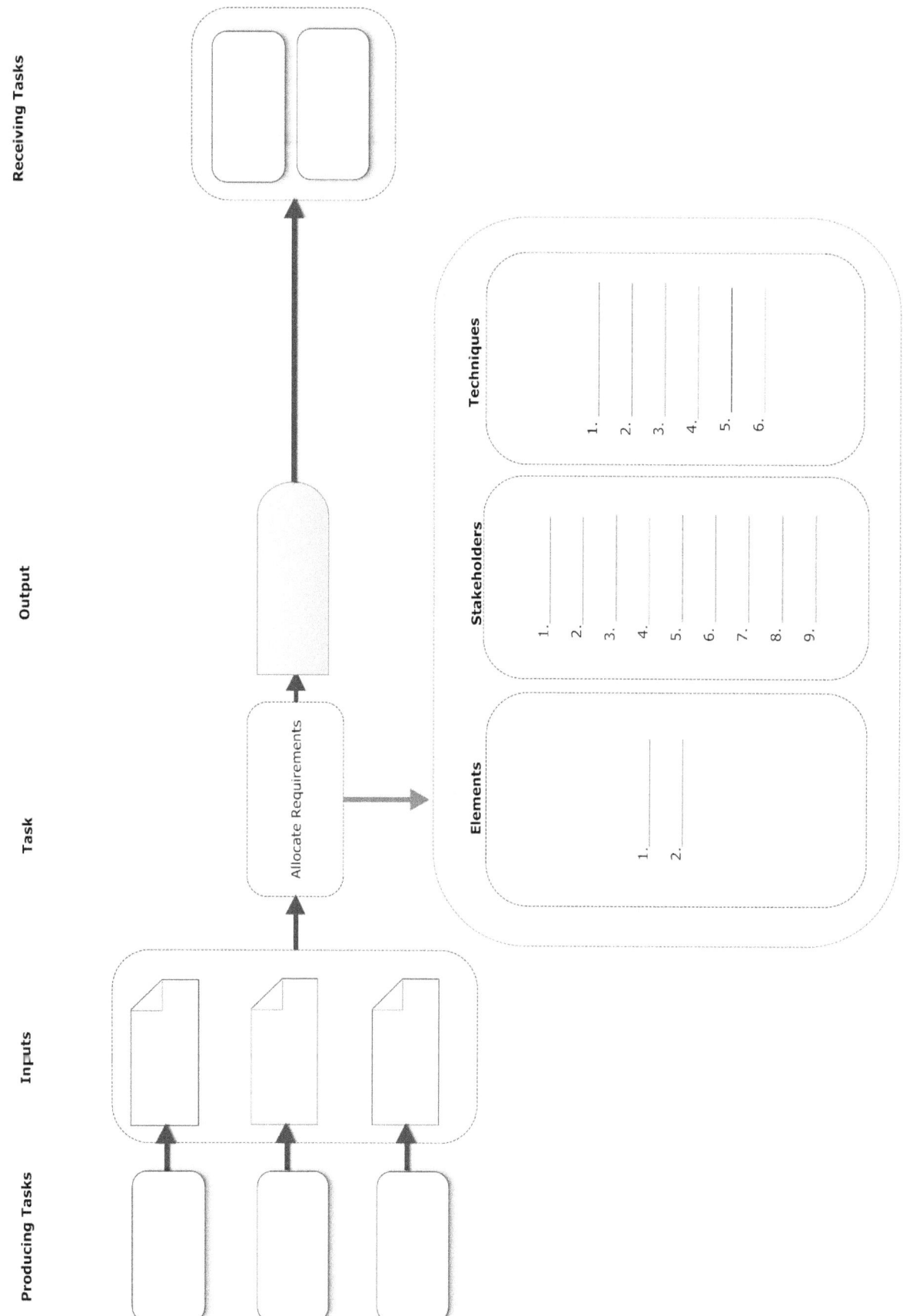

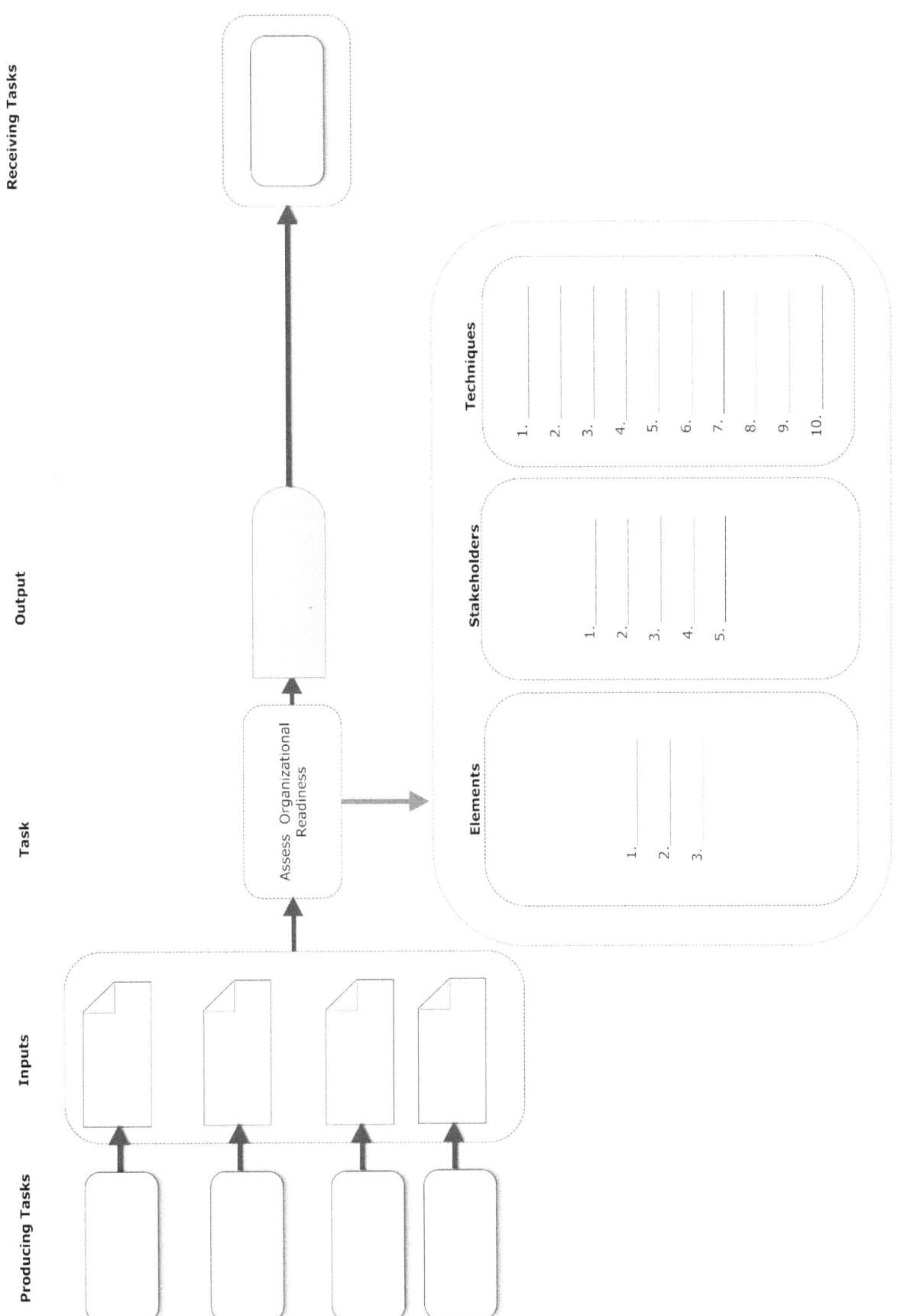

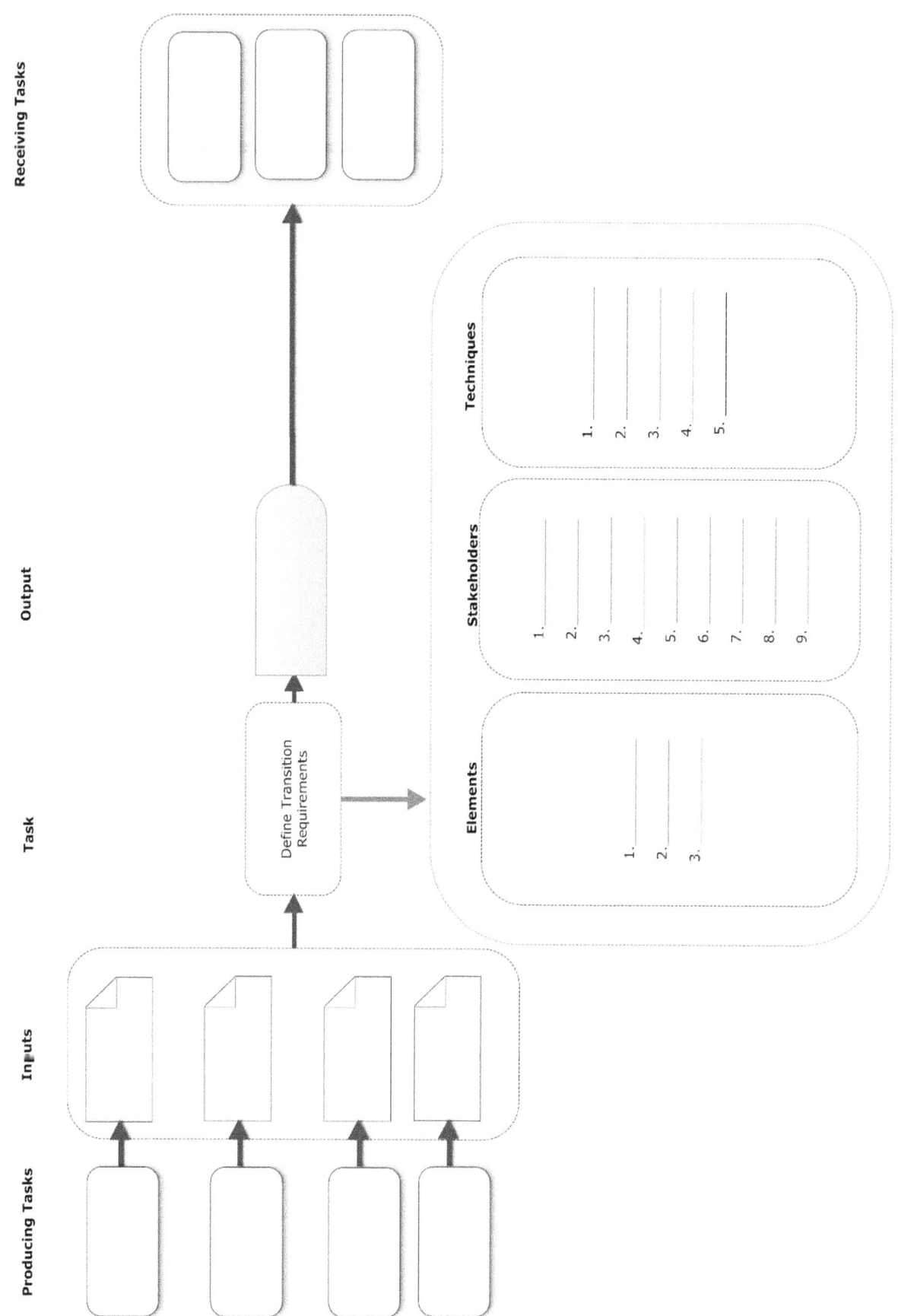

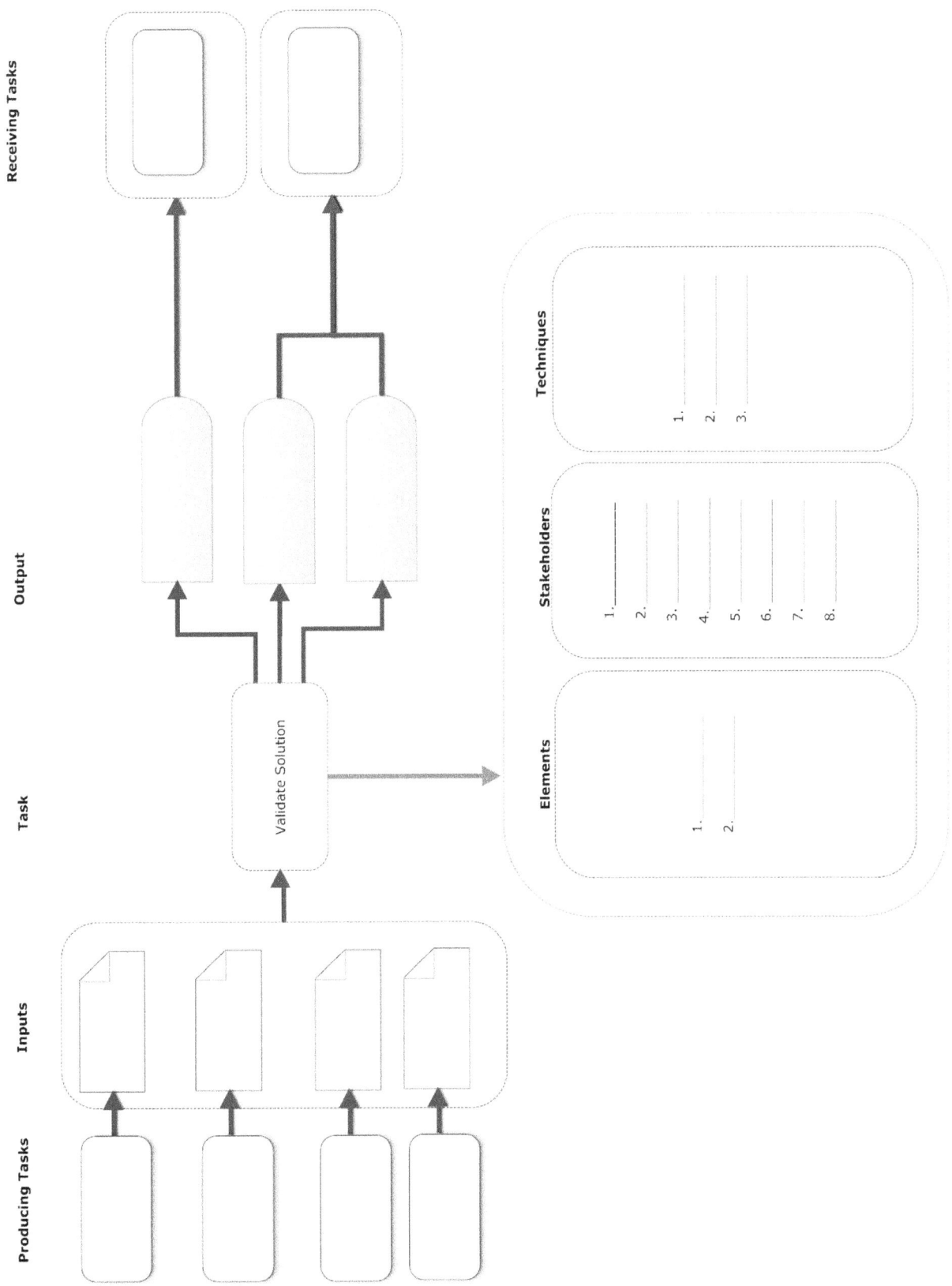

PRODUCT CATALOG
Study Aids...

BABOK® Interactive MindMap

Whether you are looking for a birds-eye view of the *BABOK® Guide, version 2.0* or a deep dive, this interactive java applet version of the *BABOK® Guide, version 2.0* will guide your understanding of the relationships between the tasks, techniques, input, outputs and elements of each knowledge area of the BABOK 2.0.

CBAP® & CCBA™ Quick Quiz Flashcards

Assess your understanding of the key terms of the *BABOK® Guide, version 2.0*.with our quick quiz flashcards. Use them to jog your memory and learn the key terms that you may encounter on IIBA® exams.

CBAP® & CCBA™ Workbook

Whether you are a visual learner or kinesthetic learner, you will find this workbook useful for gaining a better understanding of the components of each knowledge area of the *BABOK®*.
Our workbook will increase your knowledge using ITO diagrams, fill in the blanks and matching exercises, crossword puzzles, and practice questions.

Study Aids...

1 -CBAP® & CCBA™ Exam Prep Quick Study Aid

This six weeks plan and study aid is excellent for study group members and self paced learners. Whether you are studying alone or have joined a study group, this study aid will keep you on track, helps you focus and give you motivation to accomplish your goal.

Start your journey by setting your goals, creating a customized schedule, and dive into your learning.

This study aid gives you a structured outline with plenty of space to write down what you know from your learning. It contains numerous diagrams, which is great for both the visual and kinesthetic learners.

Mobile Flashcards

Take a quiz or go through *BABOK® Guide, version 2.0* key terms while waiting at a doctor's office or in line. Our mobile flashcards was designed for professionals who want to learn on the go. Using your iPhone, iPad and iPod Touch devices, Android phones and tablets, you will be able to access our terms bank and start a quiz or a flashcards exercise.

Downloadable Podcasts

In the same spirit as studying on the go, we've created podcasts for professionals who want to learn on the go. These podcasts provide you with a detailed summary of the *BABOK® Guide, version 2.0*. Listen to them often to increase your memorization and understanding.

Study Aids...

CBAP® & CCBA™ Interactive e-FlashCards

- Over 500 terms including structure of the BABOK® Guide version 2.0
- Break down of terms by knowledge area, tasks and techniques
- Image illustration of concepts
- More than just terms, also quick quizzes
- Bonus: 200+ Mobile flashcard terms

-Select from 3 study modes:
- Flashcards Mode: flip between term and definition or view both term and definition on the same card
  - Shuffle mode | Listen to cards read out | Toggle between views: term first, definition first or both on the same card
- Learn Mode: assess what you've retained
  - Prompt Term: toggle between guessing the definition or term
  - Speak it: listen to a read out of either the term or definition
  - Configuration: adjust settings for assessment
- Scatter Game Mode: game to match terms and definitions

Bulk Purchase

If you have an order of 10 or more and would like to benefit from our discounted rates, please call us: 888.856.0958 or email us at info@thebamentor.com

GetApproved® CBAP® or CCBA™ Application Tools

CBAP® & CCBA™ Application Guide Package

Our CBAP® & CCBA™ Application Guide package will help in four folds:
1. Organize your experience as required by IIBA
2. Align your experience to the qualified BA tasks (as listed in the BABOK 2.0)
3. Determine your eligibility to sit for the CBAP exam
4. Avoid the traps that could get your application denied

Package Contains:
- CBAP® or CCBA™ Application Worksheet
- CBAP® or CCBA™ Application Workshop slides/handouts
- Business Analysis Task & Deliverable Cheatsheet
- Experience Organization Worksheet

CBAP® & CCBA™ Application Worksheet

Our CBAP® & CCBA™ application worksheet will help you assess your qualification to sit for the CBAP® or CCBA™ exam, help you avoid the traps that could get your application denied and align your experience with the accepted tasks of business analysis.

Practice Questions and Exam Simulations

Exam Simulations Gain access to our large CBAP® and CCBA™ question bank. Our exam simulations and practice questions provide you with a deep dive into each knowledge area as well as a comprehensive exam imitating IIBA® exams. The deep dives questions allow you to assess your understanding of all the components of a knowledge area. These questions provide a full spectrum of questions that you can encounter on the exam.

The type of question we use to assess your knowledge are:

Question type	Assessment
Structure	Your ability to associate a given concept with the appropriate knowledge area
Content	Your ability to apply logic and solve a business analysis problem with the knowledge provided in the *BABOK® Guide, version 2.0*
Definition	Your ability to distinguish between one term versus another
Techniques	Your ability to apply business analysis techniques given a scenario
Relationship	Your ability to distinguish between two different components of the knowledge areas

Bulk Purchase

If you have an order of 10 or more and would like to benefit from our discounted rates, please call us: 888.856.0958 or email us at info@thebamentor.com

Courses & Trainings

CBAP® or CCBA™ Exam Prep Course

Six or eight weeks session of instruction either in a self paced environment or with a CBAP® certified instructor. Participants gain a tremendous number of tips and tricks to succeed on the first try.

BAMentor has a 98% success rate on IIBA® certification exams.

These courses include:
1. **24 PD** Hours (or CDUs) towards IIBA® certification (or re-certification).
2. Instructor-led **live webinar** sessions.
3. Live Chat, Q & A and short Quizzes during webinar sessions.
4. Access to **recorded** Webinar Sessions for playback.
5. Access to **Podcasts** (downloadable to your M4V or MP4 players).
6. Q & A Discussion **forums** within e-learning portal.
7. **Practice questions** that drawn from 1000+ questions with automated grading and feedback.
8. Numerous **study aids**
9. Consultation for CBAP® Application (**Application workshop**).
10. Instructor involvement via email and phone.

BABOK® Deep Dive Series

Whether you are preparing for the CBAP® or CCBA™ or simply want to learn more about the tasks and techniques of business analysis, these deep dive series will increase your knowledge of business analysis.

Not only will you learn more about the task and techniques of the *BABOK® Guide, version 2.0* you will also learn how to apply them in your day to day routine. These courses are a powerful way to increase your knowledge of business analysis standards and take your career to the next level.

These series include:
1. 7 - 12 PD Hours (or CDUs) to apply towards IIBA® certification (or recertification).
2. Pre-recorded podcast
3. Live instructor led webinar
4. Recorded instructor led webinar for review
5. Student Guide
6. How to e-booklet
7. Quick Reference guide
8. Template
9. Sample deliverable
10. Assessment of your understanding

Courses & Trainings

IIBA® Certification Application Workshops

Would you like to get your application approved on the first trial? Have you already applied and got a denial? Don't make the same mistake twice. Our application workshop will provide you all the necessary tools and

These workshops include:
1. **All your questions answered** about how to successfully apply for the CBAP® or CCBA™ in 1 to 1½ hours of instructions
2. CBAP® or CCBA™ **Application Worksheet**
3. Business Analysis Task & Deliverable Cheatsheet
4. Experience Organization Worksheet
5. **Bonus**: Sneak Peek of 3 days access to our CBAP® or CCBA™ exam practice questions to get you motivated

---

Group discounts
Our group discount rate is as follows:
2 - 3 people receive 20% off standard prices
4 - 6 people receive 25% off standard prices
7+ people receive 30% off standard prices

To benefit from these discounted rates call us: 888.856.0958 or email us at info@thebamentor.com

www.ingramcontent.com/pod-product-compliance
Lightning Source LLC
LaVergne TN
LVHW061318060426
835507LV00019B/2211